ABOUT THE AUTHOR

Following her authorship ~~of her first book, One~~ *One Dog and Her Man*, Dido, the chocolate Labrador, has achieved many firsts for dogdom. She has appeared in the Parade of Dog Personalities at Crufts and received letters of congratulation and thanks from HM the Queen and the Queen Mother for sending them copies signed with her now-famous paw-mark. Dido is the first canine author to be listed in the Authors' Catalogues of great libraries and the first to open a bank account for her royalties.

After producing seven chocolate puppies her fame has spread until she has become Britain's most publicized dog with many appearances in magazines – sometimes as covergirl – in newspapers, on television and radio. She opens fairs, fêtes and other public events, takes part in lectures explaining the uniqueness of the dog-man relationship and campaigns vigorously for the Rights of Dog.

ABOUT HER CHAP

Dido's literary 'ghost', Chapman Pincher, used to be best known for his undercover investigations into espionage but, after using his skills to penetrate the secrets of being a dog in a mainly human world, he has become something of a dogs-body. In addition to assisting Dido to record their joint findings, his duties have extended to accompanying her to distant photocalls and venues to which she has been invited as a VID, interpreting for her in media interviews and introducing her at other events. All these have burgeoned since their joint decision to produce *A Box of Chocolates*. Dido's fan mail is now prodigious and must be answered. All manner of treats, tributes and presents arrive at their joint country home in the village of Kintbury, in Berkshire, from grateful readers, even including a sonnet about her. All this has made them even more inseparable.

A BOX OF CHOCOLATES

by Dido

assisted by

CHAPMAN PINCHER

BANTAM BOOKS

LONDON · NEW YORK · TORONTO · SYDNEY · AUCKLAND

A BOX OF CHOCOLATES
A BANTAM BOOK 0 553 40717 1

First publication in Great Britain

PRINTING HISTORY
Bantam Books edition published 1993

This book is set in 10/12pt Linotype Palatino by
Phoenix Typesetting, Ilkley, West Yorkshire.

Bantam Books are published by Transworld Publishers Ltd,
61–63 Uxbridge Road, Ealing, London W5 5SA,
in Australia by Transworld Publishers (Australia) Pty Ltd,
15–25 Helles Avenue, Moorebank, NSW 2170,
and in New Zealand by Transworld Publishers (NZ) Ltd,
3 William Pickering Drive, Albany, Auckland.

Made and printed in Great Britain by
Cox & Wyman Ltd, Reading, Berks.

To chocolates – of all kinds

CONTENTS

AUTHOR'S ACKNOWLEDGEMENTS

Every man has his day

I would like to take this opportunity to thank my literary assistant, whom I call my Chap, for his patience in serving as my interpreter, for his expertise on the word processor, for his time, which he conserves so obsessively, and for putting up with the occasional temperament which, I am told, is customary for famous females of any species. I admit to being a tough task-mistress but life is short and one must press on.

He has done his best to think like a dog and take a bitch's eye view of the world. In the process I have detected something of a dog beneath his skin, which is probably why we understand each other so well. Perhaps I should also commend his courage in putting on the record without demur – at least in print – what I really think about him.

I must also express my gratitude to the Chap's wife who, for obvious reasons, I call the Boss, for her bitch-like devotion to me at all times but especially while I was producing and nursing my pups, when female sympathy and understanding were so welcome.

9

Readers have been of considerable assistance in posing queries which I have been happy to resolve and several have enhanced my fulfilment as an author by telling me that I taught them a lot which they did not know about themselves as well as about their dogs.

I make no apology for the steamy sex scenes. Indeed if the book is described as a collar-ripper I shall be delighted because nothing could be better for the sales.

Dido,
Kintbury, Berks.
January 1993

Foreword by the Chap

Beware of the dog

I never imagined that I would literally become a dogs-body, defined by my dictionary as a drudge, but that has been my fate since I agreed to assist my chocolate Labrador, Dido, to record her views about the 'canine predicament' in a book aptly entitled *One Dog and Her Man*. No book I have authored on my own account has provoked such a reader response and I have been required to spend more time dealing with her fan mail than with my own correspondence. I have also gravitated to the role of chauffeur, minder and, with the spate of dog-napping, bodyguard, when she fulfils her numerous publicity appearances and charitable duties arising out of her fame.

Nor have I ever received so many requests for a further volume as Dido has. Having more serious projects on hand, I manfully resisted the pressures from Dido and her supporters to set aside the time required but she, and they, were so determined that I was dogdozed into it, especially when she wrote such a compelling title by giving birth to a splendid litter of seven chocolate puppies in a large, oak whelping box.

In truth, though, my sojourn in down-to-earth dog-dom has been a salutary relief from the *demi-monde* of traitors and spies, for it is a cleaner world where there is no treachery, no deception and 'dirty tricks' do not exist while trust, love and straightforwardness abound.

1 My Life as a Celebrity

Fame is the cur

I knew that I had joined the ranks of the famous authors when a letter addressed to 'Dido, Kintbury, Berks' reached me with no delay. Since then, there have been several other letters and small parcels containing treats addressed, 'Dido, care of the Chap, Kintbury, Berks'. They all made it. More often they are addressed to 'Miss Dido Chapman Pincher' and I have even had 'Lady Di'. The letter which I rate most highly was from Her Majesty the Queen but I will reserve that story for a later chapter. I had fan letters from other important people, some sent from foreign countries as far away as America, New Zealand, Australia and South Africa. Friends travelling abroad send me wish-you-were-here cards. Indeed, my fan mail has reached such proportions, especially since the paperback of *One Dog and Her Man* emerged, that the Chap has begun to bleat about it, complaining that the dog is wagging the man because I am taking up too much of his time, though I can't think of any way in which it could be occupied to better purpose. After all, he is benefitting from my labours, intellectually as well as financially, and why

13

keep a man and bark? Actually, he is more punctilious about answering my letters than his own.

I have to agree with him that when people write asking for my photograph it can become a bit expensive, as it does when they want books signed by both of us as prizes for tombolas, raffles and competitions. It can also be a problem when my fans bring their books to the house for signature when he is otherwise engaged. Heaven knows what will happen when this new book reaches the stalls. Queues outside the house?

Naturally, most people who bought my book wanted it signed by the author – in fact by both authors. The only way I could sign was with a paw-print but, clearly, there were going to be problems if my paw had to be daubed with ink and plonked on every book. Apart from the fact that some books might get spoiled there was the danger that I might get writer's cramp, wear out my paw or develop RSI – Repetitive Strain Injury – for which so many people are now claiming compensation from their employers.

Fortunately, the problems were solved, brilliantly, by a local dentist, Dr Richard Charon of Newbury, assisted by his pretty wife, Chris, and his dental assistant, Katie. The Chap took me to his surgery and we left the car in a nearby car-park with an hour on the ticket which the Chap, being a canny northerner, thought would be enough. Though we were only in the waiting-room I detected a slight antiseptic smell about it and feared that I might be at another vet's but I realized that I wasn't when they all made such a fuss and started feeding me with Jaffa Cakes.

As I had stated in my book that I was right-handed the print had to be of my right, front paw otherwise discerning readers would realize that I had signed their books with the wrong one. All three mixed some goo normally used for dental impressions and my paw was firmly plonked into a bowl-full of it with the Chap, and everyone else there, assuring me that there was nothing to fear, though dentists always say that, I am told. I didn't mind much, so long as the Jaffa Cakes kept coming, but they pressed my paw down so deeply that it went down to the bottom and the imprint was ruined when I was released. After a conference they decided to have another try, which meant more Jaffa Cakes. An extra-large mix of dental-impression material was prepared and my paw was put into it, more gently this time. A perfect mould of my paw was produced and this was immediately filled with a mix of synthetic polymer rubber, normally reserved for human patients having highly intricate crowns and bridges made for their own canines. When this had set it was mounted on a handle to make a paw-stamp which could be quickly pressed into a brown ink-pad and then printed on to a page of the book to give a permanent pawtograph.

At that moment I became probably the only dog to have a false paw as well as four real ones. Also I had probably made canine history in another way. There can be few other dogs who have been taken to a human dentist's surgery for treatment. Later, they also made a framed replica of the paw for the Chap, which is on his study wall and another one which is on display in the waiting-room. Collectors' pieces of the future, perhaps?

As so often happens with the Chap, the pantomime was not over. When we got back to the car-park the hour had been over-run and the attendant had spotted it. To avoid a fine the Chap tried to explain that he had been unexpectedly held up at the dentist's. 'What! With a dog!' was the incredulous response. Then, of course, the attempt to explain that we had both been there in connection with a book I had written sounded even more far-fetched. We got away with paying for an extra hour largely, I suspect, because the attendant thought he might be dealing with a nut and wanted rid of him.

The pawtograph has been a great success and when bookshops started asking us to sign copies the Chap devised a refinement. He bought a lot of sticky bookplates, put the imprint on those along with his own signature and sent them off by post. The joke was that when he had to do fifty at a time he got stamper's wrist and could not understand what was causing the pain. It has been worth every twinge, I reckon, for star quality deserves star treatment. He has had to do hundreds for the paperback and now that my book is being translated into German for publication in Germany maybe we shall have to practise signing, '*Mit liebe von Dido*'. Not very good German, I am told, but I only bark one language. How I will cope with the sales in Japan, where I have also sold the rights, I simply don't know. Should I sign it 'Honourable Dido' with '*Banzai!*' instead of 'Best wishes'? Anything to become a yen millionairess!

When people doubt that I am really the author the Chap has a convincing reply. He tells them how he looked me up in the D section of the Authors' catalogue at the London Library and there, along with Charles Dickens, Daniel Defoe, and Conan Doyle, is Dido. Further, the copy of my book on the shelves has a London Library bookplate stating 'Presented by Chapman Pincher and Dido'. As the Chap says, 'What can't bark can't lie.' Now my appetite has been whetted I am hoping to get so many more books in the catalogue that, as far as I am concerned, it will be a dogalogue. I certainly hope to get as many as the Chap, who has quite a few listed there. I suppose I could say that I look on the Chap as my Boswell. A pity I can't preface my pronouncements with 'Sir'!

My first book is already in *Who's Who* through the Chap's entry there and I feel confident that if there was a *Who's Woof* I would be in it on my own account. *Publications* would present no difficulty. Neither would *Recreations* – fishing and baiting the Chap. I could even cope with the part on the entry form which says *Clubs* – in my case Kennel and Labrador.

When the Chap and the Boss were invited to the party to celebrate the reopening of Hatchards, the prestigious bookshop in Piccadilly, copies of my book were on display – not in the Pets or Animals section but in Biography! If that isn't one-updogship then I don't know what is. Later, when the Authors of the Year party was held there, the nice Mr Geoffrey Bailey, who organized the invitations, said I should have gone because I had a right to, having made the bestseller list, but the Boss thought I might get trodden on. Still, it would have been another first for dogdom and I should have taken the risk.

The Chap suggested that to avoid any accusation of being 'politically incorrect' they should send me my own invitation in future, but the security men were worried about such a valuable dog being injured in a crush of 300 authors. So, at the 1993 party, reporters who wanted to interview me were told that I had dogcotted it and that, to make amends, Hatchards had promised me a signing session for this book – a unique distinction for a dog.

As another token of my literary status, my publisher and public relations officer travelled all the way from London to see me, more than once. All but the top-flight authors have to go to London to see them.

When an author is visited at home by her publisher she can be said to have arrived. My paperback publishers also visited me at my home bringing some show-cards showing the cover with me on it and headed 'Local Author', meaning me, of course.

Still, the peak of my public honours, to date, was my selection by the Kennel Club to appear in the Parade of Dog Personalities before all the *dognoscenti* at Cruft's in January 1992, an unforgettable highlight of my career which I will also deal with more fully in a later chapter. Suffice it to record here that the local paper, the *Newbury Weekly News*, headlined the event with 'Literary dog to be honoured by Cruft's'.

I can date my fame from Monday 14 January 1991, the day when the *Daily Mail* began to serialize my first book. The newspaper had sent their ace animal photographer, Mike Hollist, who took literally hundreds of pictures. He is such a nice man that I didn't mind doing anything he asked and the results were superb, even by my exacting standards, as they showed me in all sorts of circumstances without detracting from the dignity of dog, which so many newspaper photographs do. It was, in fact, the Chap's dignity which was to be assailed to an extent which made him splutter.

The contract with the *Daily Mail* stipulated that the Chap and I would help to promote the series on television. The advertising agency wanted me to sit in a chair answering questions, which I was more than happy to do, but when they told the Chap what his function would be I thought the old fellow was going to have apoplexy. To round off the action of the TV trailer, which was to be shown nationwide, several times at peak hours, they wanted to photograph him on all fours with a copy of the *Daily Mail* in his mouth! He is not unduly self-conscious but I knew he would never agree to such a blow to his dignity. Besides, he was about to publish a serious book about political dirty tricks and felt that such an abasement would be a dirty trick on his image.

Fortunately the agency agreed to try again and eventually telephoned to say that they did not need either of us. We were duly astonished when the trailer appeared on our television screen with what looked exactly like me sitting in a leather chair answering questions, especially when the dog replied 'Yes' when asked if she had a low opinion of some human beings. At short notice the agency had found another chocolate Labrador bitch, called Jay, to serve as my stand-in and the only give-away was her brown leather collar because I always wear yellow. She certainly upheld the Labrador reputation for high intelligence because she had never been in a TV studio before. When Jay was asked, among other things, if she was outspoken about her owner she appeared to reply, 'Nobody's perfect.' The whole studio team collapsed in laughter. It was really Jay's day and I suppose that she could be described as a real copy-dog. Still, imitation is the sincerest form of flattery and having a stand-in is a sure sign of real stardom. Jay, with whom I correspond and who is now a friend, is a bitch after my own heart.

Later we learned how she had been made to talk like a human. She happened to have been trained to bark whenever shown a bowl of food. So she was shown the bowl several times while being photographed on the TV camera. Then, later, instead of the sound of her barks, they added human speech, spoken by an actor, as she opened and closed her mouth. I must say that it was very effective and everybody assumed that it was I who was speaking as they do with a film star for whom someone else is singing.

So, like Byron, I awoke one morning and found myself famous. The *Daily Mail* series, which ran for three days with lots of colour pictures of me, the Chap and the Boss, started off my scrapbook of cuttings and photographs which is already getting quite fat. Also, an artist has painted my portrait and it really looks like me while the portrait of the Chap, painted by John Bratby, looks like some village idiot with big ears. One dear old lady even embroidered a cushion with my head on it which everyone admires when they spot it.

There was the usual excitement when the proofs of *One Dog and Her Man* came and then advance copies of the book, with a colour photograph of both of us on the front and a nice portrait of my head on the back. Publication day was supposed to be in May but there were delays and problems getting books into the shops, due to what the Chap calls 'the slings and arrows of outrageous publishers'.

As soon as the book appeared I was invited by the BBC to appear on the *Gloria Live* television show to be interviewed by Gloria Hunniford at Lime Grove, while millions would be watching. The Chap, who says he never thought that he would end his professional career as a ghost-writer to a dog, is also my minder so he had to be in on the act. It was my début in a studio and the first thing we did was to go into the make-up room. The Chap needed it – for a start he has no eyebrows – but I didn't. Gloria described my performance as 'very professional' and there was plenty of applause from the studio audience, though I gather that is not always as sincere as it sounds. Some other dogs were brought into the programme and some of them whined but I didn't.

My next TV performance, when the TVS *Coast to Coast* programme covered the opening of my bank account, was so demanding that I will deal with it in connection with my financial affairs. With such experiences, I soon became something of a TV caninity and am now quite an old paw at it. With my garrulous minder always beside me I'll never 'corpse', as they say about people who dry up on TV.

It was the same with the radio. We did fifteen programmes, including the *Derek Jameson Show*, which was nationwide early in the morning. Derek was once the Chap's editor on the *Daily Express*, so they were old friends and he was very nice to me. So was Peter White, a blind man who runs a chat show on Radio Solent. We were on the air with him in the Southampton studio for several minutes before the Chap realized that our interviewer was reading from notes in Braille. He knew more about our book and asked more penetrating questions than any of the others and was most charming to me.

Although the radio audiences could neither see nor hear me, the Chap always insisted on having the senior author present. He said it gave him confidence to have me by his side. Dido and the Chap! It sounds like a knockabout turn! Some of the programmes sent us tape recordings and I sat with my couple as they listened, perking up when I heard my name. We did so many radio programmes 'down the line' from the BBC studio in Oxford, where they always make a fuss of me, that the Boss said they must have eventually thought, as we entered the door, 'Here comes that silly old sod again with his dog.' I've been to Oxford so many times now that I think I have earned an honorary degree – a dogtorate perhaps of Brazenose College because nobody can doubt that I have plenty of brass nerve.

After the first week of sales my book was up to eleventh on *The Sunday Times* bestseller list. If I could have got into the Top Ten, with that Professor Hawking, I should have had bones coming out of my ears! I didn't quite make it but my book also sold well to public libraries and has become the most stolen book from several hotels. All this shows that I am not just a pretty face and maybe this book will do even better.

In newspaper stories and reviews I was subjected to headlines like 'Barking all the way to the bank' and 'Bone idol', 'Man writes dog' and even 'La donna e mobile'. My friend, Kenneth Rose, wrote a nice item about me and the Chap in his 'Albany' column in the *Sunday Telegraph*. When the paper arrived and the Chap saw that my photograph and his appeared side by side in it he called up the stairs to the Boss, who was still in bed, 'We've both got our pictures in the paper.' Naturally, she thought 'both' meant her and she was not best pleased when she came down and found that it didn't. She reckons that incident settled, beyond doubt, who is really the First Lady of our house. That marks the achievement of only a small ambition, though, when my aim is to be the First Lady of Dogdom or, at least, the First Bitch of Grub Street. I suppose that being a Cover Girl, as I was, in colour, on the front cover of *Country Magazine*, was a further step in that direction. I may get a reputation of being a publicity hound but I can take that so long as it keeps coming.

With my book selling like hot biscuits I was asked to open fêtes and bazaars and have even opened an extension to a school. I was described in the local paper as 'equally as famous' as the Chap, which I considered to be something of an underestimate. I have also been involved in lectures at places like health farms, where I am needed to prompt the Chap in case he dries up. So far I have done all these things for nothing, though sometimes I get a present of a few treats. But human stars get a fee for this kind of service so perhaps I need an agent. The Chap's hopeless about money. I shall have to take him more firmly in paw on this matter.

I have also taken part in a mass presentation to book-sellers when my paperback publishers, Transworld, put on one of their Roadshows at the Hilton Hotel in Bristol. There I was, an honoured authoress, on the big screen with Catherine Cookson, Jilly Cooper, Danielle Steel and Frederick Forsyth. I had been given permission to sit in at the dinner so that we could move round tables and meet as many people as possible. Of course, the Chap was there too – to introduce me. A chauffered car had been specially sent for me and I let the Chap and the Boss come too. There were high hopes, as well as high hypes, for big paperback sales and I may even sell in the schools. With left-wing crackpots eliminating William Shakespeare from the reading syllabus in schools and putting in texts like *Neighbours* and *Allo! Allo!* I don't see why they shouldn't include my book. At least it would help to ensure that the young are brought up to be 'politically correct' about the place of dogs in the scheme of things.

As any star will tell you, such promotional events, like photo-calls, soon become boring, but they are an essential part of the profession of author these days. There is also the principle of *noblesse oblige* and I feel that with all the bad publicity to which my species has been subjected, especially in connection with so-called 'killer dogs', I must seize every opportunity to upgrade the image of dog. There is also a log of gratuitously perjorative misuses of our name to overcome such headlines like 'Bad Debts Dog Banks', phrases like 'buying a pup' and horrid expressions like 'dog ends' and 'looking like a dog's dinner', which is how the Chap describes himself when the Boss makes him dress up in topper and tails to take her to Ascot races.

So, each day I am ready for whatever is next on our agenda. Since becoming famous I never have much time on my paws. However, I must be careful to avoid over-exposure because to be over-praised is to court disaster in this country, as the media and the public will eventually turn on you and savage you. As one of the Chap's successful business pals put it, in my presence, 'If you put your head above the parapet in this country there is always someone waiting to knock it off.' Sound advice but it has not deterred me from accepting journalistic commissions, my first being for the Christmas number of the *Shooting Times* on what it is like being a dog in a shooting line. This was another first, and I also review books about dogs. With the book trade the way it is, we authors need to top up our incomes with what I suppose is hack work. I don't mind being the first canine hack.

The joint lives of our pack are full of surprises, these days. For example, when I was standing relaxing with the Chap at a big open-air wedding reception, a couple came up and said, 'Is that Dido?' They had recognized me by my chocolate colour and my bright yellow collar, which is now my logo though I got it, originally, because otherwise in dim light I'm the invisible dog and the rest of the pack trips over me. They had not recognized the Chap. People now say to him, 'Are you the man who owns that famous dog?' and he replies, a little glumly I think, 'No. She owns me.' Sometimes they stop us in the street and ask, 'Is that the famous Dido?' Especially if they happen to have heard him calling me. Dido may be a silly-sounding name but, like the Chap's, which is even dafter, people do remember it.

One elderly man who heard the Chap calling my name on the canal tow-path said, 'That's interesting! My wife's name is Dido.'

'After the Queen who founded Carthage?' the Chap asked.

'Yes. We celebrated our tenth wedding anniversary by going all the way there just to see it.'

'Was it worth it?' asked the Chap.

'No. There was nothing there,' the old fellow replied sadly.

It was a romantic gesture but romantic is not quite the right word to apply to anything to do with Carthage. The Romans levelled it to the ground after they got fed up with Hannibal and his elephants, while Dido herself also came to a sticky end, which I intend to avoid.

The Chap is now resigned to these sorts of encounters and takes them very well, on the whole, but I am not sure that he was best pleased when the publishers of the paperback version of *One Dog and Her Man* sent him the advance copy of the cover. I had pushed him off the front, which is perhaps the worst thing you can do to an old journalist. Instead of the photograph of the two of us in the garden, which had graced the front cover of the hardback edition, there was only me on one of my favourite chairs in the sitting room. Still, he should know by now that authorship has its trials as well as its joys.

I imagine he might have been slightly miffed when an American admirer wrote a lovely poem about me, because nobody of any nationality has ever expressed their admiration of the Chap in verse. In my first book I remarked that 'I would like to be the dark bitch of somebody's sonnet' and in October 1992 a sonnet arrived by post from a learned denizen of Illinois, called Bill Bourland, whom I had met while walking in our village. He and his wife were visiting Kintbury and came in to see my puppies. Here are his immortal lines, entitled '*Ad Canem Femina Fusca et Lepida*', meaning 'To a dog, female, dark and charming':

Along the Lido, Dido, let us stroll.
You are to me as Laura to Petrarch,
Helen to Paris, Shakespeare's lady dark.
You are an inspiration to my soul!
I love your chocolate coat (a stylish stole),
I love your silken ears, your noble bark –
To me a sound as sweet as any lark.
(How I would love to hear you bark a role!)
I will have died, O Dido, should you die –
The Dog Star will have vanished from my sky.
But you're alive – making the whole world bright,
Your Carthaginian brood such a delight!
The world may deem me poor, but I am rich
Because I've met you: charming chocolate bitch.

My poet annotated his lines with paw-notes explaining, among other matters, that it would be, naturally, in *The Tales of Hoffdogg* that he would love to hear me bark a role. To that, of course, my immediate response was, 'No problem! I Offenbach'.

What female could fail to be deeply touched by such a romantic tribute, especially as we had met for such a short time? It was like that lovely old song about a man seeing a lady passing by yet loving her until he should die.

Like most things, fame is said to have its price. So what penalties have I paid? The Boss says that fame has made me into something of a prima dogga, and others in the village have accused me of having a 'star temperament', but I don't think it has changed

26

me much though it has changed the attitude of people towards me. They seem more deferential. Not the Chap, though. He tries to dilute my fame by saying that, like great men, great dogs do not obey the laws of optics – the nearer you get to them the smaller they become. Ah well, a dog is not without honour save in its own pack!

One major penalty for me is having to keep a trim figure in case I have to make a personal appearance or do photo-calls. The Boss sees that I do not overeat and slims me down if my beam begins to broaden. It will be a continuous battle because, while fame is supposed to be the spur, as I suspect it is with the Chap, for me, food will always be a much greater incentive. Fortunately, I am unlikely to be beset with the problems of ageing, as women are, for we bitches grow old much more gracefully and less obviously. Still, ageing is less important for a writer than for a show dog. Female writers of all species are permitted to grow old gracefully. They say that fame is the thirst of youth but I sense that I would like it to continue. It all depends on whether I can stay on the ladder. Dogs are not really built for ladders.

The Chap claims that he is the one who has paid the penalties for my fame, being reduced to being my adoguensis, minder and just an appendage. He says that I now dominate his life through the Dido Industry and has published articles describing his predicament. The dog is wagging the man so much that one of our mutual friends suggested that he should form an organization called CLAWS – Chocolate Labrador Assistant Writers' Society. I like it! He should have heeded the old advice never to act with animals – not only because things can go wrong but because we are such scene-stealers. Seriously, though, there's no escape for him now. An authoress must stay in close touch with her ghost and one can't change ghost writers in mid-flow.

2 A Dog She Would A-wooing Go

The best laid plans of dogs and men . . .

On 26 September 1992 I was brought back to earth from my literary fantasies with a bang – seven bangs, in fact – as I shall now relate.

In the summer of the previous year, Mrs Susan Towers-Clark, who has bred chocolate Labradors for more than forty years, staged a field day exclusively for chocolates in a pasture round her home, Greatworth Manor, which is a lovely old place on a hill not far from Brackley, in Northamptonshire. There were fifty-one chocolate dogs – one of the biggest collections of chocolates in history. At one stage, so many seemed to be arriving at once that it looked as though there could be a dog-jam. Happily it was a sunny day, and there were lots of lovely scents to follow once I was allowed off my lead, and I encountered so many of my kind that I became quite confused because, usually, at any gathering of dogs I am the odd-girl-out so far as colour is concerned and am immediately recognizable.

The Chap and the Boss are forever worrying that I might get overweight, but compared to some of those who turned up I was as slim as a herring. When I saw what they looked like I could see the Boss's point. Unfortunately, as I have admitted, the favourite pastime of all Labradors, including me, is eating and always will be.

My most fateful meeting was with Bugler, Mrs Towers-Clark's famous stud dog, a real noseful, very handsome and almost exactly the same age as me. So everyone thought that we should make a good match one day. One of the Towers-Clark's chocolate bitches had just produced a lovely litter of ten chocolate pups which set me alight, or at any rate made the Boss feel broody. It would be a consummation devoutly to be wished some time in the future, the Chap agreed, being in a literary mood. There was an older sire on offer in a village much closer to home but we all wanted a young husband. None of us was for a sugar-daddy, even a chocolate one.

As with many another career girl, my professional obligations had to be given priority over my sex life. The instinctive attraction of the patter of tiny paws had to give way to the commercial realities of publishing promotion. So when it was apparent that I was coming into season at the height of my various public appearances in support of my first book, especially at Sandringham, the vet gave me an injection to suppress my problem. I suppose it was a kind of canine contraceptive and no doubt there will be others as the dog population increases. (The imagination boggles.) Anyway the injection served its purpose but, as so often happens when Nature is interfered with, there may have been unforeseen consequences.

A few months later, after much discussion between the rest of the pack and the vet, it was decided that it would be in everyone's interest if I had a litter of chocolate pups without further delay, and definitely with

Bugler – Downfarm Bugler to give him his full name – as the chocolate sire. Of course, care had been taken to study our pedigrees and ensure that we were not closely related. In fact, we were not related at all and there would be no need for the ritual command about consanguinity – 'Bark now or forever hold your peace.'

However, before the seismic step could be safely taken it was necessary for me to have my hips tested and I had to undergo an X-ray examination to make sure that they were sound. Unfortunately, some members of the Labrador breed have become tainted with a bad gene which means that their hip bones do not fit securely in their sockets. As a result, they can become weak at the hips and lame as they get older. The only way to get rid of this gene, so that it is not inherited, is to ensure that dogs which are badly affected by it do not breed and pass it on to further generations. All this sounded reasonable, especially as I had no doubt about my hips, until I learned that I had to be given a general anaesthetic – made unconscious while the vet made the X-ray pictures. The trouble is that they have to make so many pictures with pin-point accuracy showing various angles of the hip-joints that no dog, least of all me, could stay still long enough. So, as the Chap put it, I had to be put out for the count. I did not enjoy it and though Julian, the vet, and his assistants were very kind, I felt wobbly for quite a while. In fact, it took me two whole days to get over it completely. Fortunately, my 'hips-scores' were very good so I won't have to go through that again.

The only nice thing was being picked up by the Chap in the evening. We were absolutely delighted to see each other and I understand he had been very worried until he heard that I had come round safely. Confidentially, he is so scared of general anaesthetics himself that when he had to have two hernias repaired he insisted on having a local. Most of his friends thought he was crazy.

Whether or not I would come into heat was something on which, for once, I held the whip-paw. Eventually I did, but later than expected because the injection I mentioned earlier had upset my rhythm. There was a count-down to my wedding day which should have been on Boxing Day but, of course, the Chap was shooting then and so, it happened, was Bugler. As a result it had to be postponed until 28 December which both the vet – examining my rear end without so much as a by your leave – and Bugler's owner judged to be propitious. Meanwhile, of course, every precaution had to be taken so that I could not get out and be subjected to a gang-bang by the village Dog Juans, who, in human terms, might also be called the Wandering Paw Gang. Considering the much-vaunted wit of man I am surprised that nobody has invented a chastity belt for dogs. If anybody has I have never seen one.

First in the field of hopeful local suitors, as always, was a persistent Jack Russell which the Chap calls 'Charmed-Life' Charlie, because he is allowed to roam the village and takes his life in his paws – perhaps I should say his legs – every time he races along the streets. He invariably gets my scent first and the Chap regards his arrival outside our back door as the first sign that I am about to be interesting. When the Chap examines me there is usually nothing to see and he swears that Charlie has a calendar. However he manages to do it, he appears with his nose under the gap of the double garden doors, apparently pondering the possibility that he might get something else under it. Admiring his enterprise, I lay down too on the other side, for most girls encourage admirers, even if they happen to be small. After all, some beautiful girls even marry jockeys. I sometimes wonder if I am like those large women who go for little men. The Chap says there is something about small males but he won't tell me what it is.

After ensuring, yet again, that anything dangerous was truly impossible through such a narrow gap – he always recalls that love laughs at locksmiths – the Chap decided to use Charlie as a teaser, as racehorse breeders do, to keep me interested until my wedding day. He doesn't mind giving Charlie a cheap thrill, any more than I do, in fact I rather enjoy it. We dogs are not snobs but he is getting a bit too old for me, though, as the Chap says, perhaps with himself in mind, 'There's many a good tune played on an old Stradivarius.' However, he did not take such a tolerant view when Charlie, in sheer frustration, had a go at the Chap's legs when he went up to the post-box. No doubt my perfume was lingering about him and set Charlie alight.

Neither Charlie nor any other would-be suitors keeping vigil outside the gate indulge in dogerwauling which is fortunate for them with the Chap's knobbly thumbstick or a bucket of water always handy.

Eventually, after the Christmas festivities, which I always enjoy because the grandchildren come, we set out on the journey to Greatworth Manor, with the Chap telling me that my number was up, whatever that was supposed to mean. I suppose he should have put a white bow on the car but he forgot.

Once I saw Bugler again, who seemed so tall, chocolate and handsome, it was love at first sniff for both of us and he couldn't have been keener to consummate the union. Neither could I – in principle. The Chap 'gave me away' and the Boss was the best-woman, as she usually is. I was let loose in the garden with

Bugler to advice from the Chap – 'Stand still and think of dogdom.' It was understood that no photographs of my mating would be taken. The last thing I want for my image as a serious author is pictures of me appearing in some pornographic magazine just as my international reputation is gathering momentum.

When I began racing round the garden, with Bugler in pursuit, expectations were raised but not much else. His advances were, literally, a more gripping experience than I had anticipated and I declined to stand still for him. We were then switched to the paddock, where we could run even further in greater privacy, and when this also proved negative we were shut in a loose box. By that stage I had given him such a run-around that all he seemed to want was a roll in the wood shavings. As a last resort we were allowed a frolic in the kitchen while the Chap, the Boss and Bugler's owner, who were more exhausted than I was, had coffee, and though he nearly got me there he didn't quite because I was still protecting my assets. It was almost, literally, a kitchen-sink drama but I was not going to part with my virginity in such unromantic surroundings.

The trouble was that I was in love with him but I wasn't minded to stand still and think of dogdom, or anything else, while he made his pelvic thrusts. There was some talk of holding me but it was generally agreed that it would constitute rape and would be unfair. So, by midday, it had come to nothing and the humans were more bored with the proceedings than we were. They were also cold, while Bugler and I had our fur coats on and were panting. It was therefore unanimously decided that there should be a break to let Bugler recover his breath or whatever else he needed to get back. (I suspect he had been worked too hard on the previous day when he was picking up pheasants. Being an excellent retriever, perhaps he was more interested in pheasants than in sex, like the Chap sometimes used to be.)

To fill in the time our party went a couple of miles along the road to see Sulgrave Manor, where George Washington's ancestors lived, partly because there is a belief in the Chap's family that they were related to the early Washingtons, who lived in Durham in a village called Wessington, of which Washington is a corruption. I was not allowed in, which was daft because there must have been dogs in the great hall when the house was built in about 1560. (On the front door there are the arms of Queen Elizabeth I supposedly supported by a lion and a dragon but the dragon looks just like a dog.)

'Once more unto the breech,' the Chap demanded after we returned to the manor house. We tried the garden, the paddock, the field and the loose box all over again but by that time all Bugler wanted was another roll in the shavings, often with me on top. Bugler had blown it because I had tired him out and overdone the hard-to-get act. I did my best to say I was sorry and felt better about things but, for him, the magic moment had passed. Serves me right, I suppose, except that he didn't serve me.

They decided to give us both a twenty-four-hour rest for a Sunday restart. I was quite exhausted by it all and slept all the way back home. As the Chap announced the sad truth, lugubriously, to our neighbours, who were expectant, when I wasn't, as we arrived back home – 'Dido wouldn't.'

Next day the Chap took me all the way back to try once more, the Boss being too tired to face it all again. I felt a lot keener but Bugler wasn't. Whatever it was that has to gel in the chemistry of love just didn't. Our magic moment had gone. I made all the running but our run-around was platonic in spite of my efforts to stimulate him. Perhaps he was paying me out for the previous day or, maybe, I had given him a disturbed night. Anyway, I thought Bugler had sounded the last post, so far as I was concerned. Instead, as an ultimate resort, it was agreed that we should try once more on my home ground in the hope that third time would be lucky. If it wouldn't work at his place, why not try mine?

I was certainly game to give it another whirl. So, on the third day, 30 December, Bugler was brought all the way over to Kintbury. The Chap cleared the lawn for action, removing any 'obstacles', some of them dog-made. Bugler duly arrived and I sensed his presence before his mistress knocked on the door. We were both warned that it just had to be 'bull's-eye' this time but for half an hour it looked as though it was going to be a repeat non-performance. Bugler seemed only interested in staking out his claim to my garden, being intent on anointing every post and bush. As his master had been a distinguished army officer, no doubt he had heard the axiom that time spent on reconnaissance is seldom wasted. He then lay down and started chewing one of my bones which I thought was hardly a compliment. I didn't bark, at least not audibly, because one must bark low if one barks love. I didn't even begrudge him the bone but it is usually the female who receives the ceremonial present, both in animal and human court-ship. Any dog who would rather attend to a bone than to me has no sense of proportion and the Boss chose to recall how the Chap had behaved in a similar, ungallant fashion. On their first evening together in Ireland on a salmon-fishing trip, he had attended to his baits instead of to her. He made up for it later, however, so it was thought that Bugler might too.

Eventually, the humans left us locked out in the garden to have their lunch, with one of them looking out of the window every few minutes. Bugler was sitting down and I seemed to be telling him what to do and even how to do it by getting on his back. Somehow, when I was least expecting it and nobody was looking, the mood seized him and he seized me. The chemistry had worked and the magic moment had arrived. The emission was accomplished.

Glancing through the window the Chap gave a triumphant cry, 'They're knotted!' Even though they were only halfway through their mince pies, everyone rushed out and I was damned glad to see them as I did not like my predicament at all. Through some extraordinary agility on Bugler's part, we were end to end, backwards, and it was anything but pleasant. I have heard about being attached to somebody but that was ridiculous. I've also heard of marriage ties but that was carrying it too far, for my taste, or rather, my feeling. If that was holy dog-knot, I did not like it at all.

Being unable to move without pain I was comforted by the Boss at my front end, with the Chap at the rear, while Bugler's mistress sympathized with her dog in what looked like his painful position. If Mrs Towers-Clark could be described as the stud groom for the occasion, then I suppose that the Chap qualified as the head lad.

It seemed an eternity, but was probably no longer than five minutes which the Chap whiled away by telling coarse jokes. One of them was about two taxis which were stuck bumper to bumper outside the Savoy in London. One passer-by suggested that they should throw a bucket of water over them, which was something that used to be done, cruelly, to dogs caught locked in the street.

Then, suddenly, we were free. Whether it was due to something that had happened to me or to him I did not know or care. All I knew was that I was no longer encumbranced by 70 pounds of flaked-out dog. If that was the honeymoon it was long enough though, looking back on the performance, I suppose it was fun, if rather overrated, the anticipation being more rewarding than the achievement. As some human said, it is better to travel rather than to arrive.

Confident that I would have a tray of chocolate buns in the oven, the Chap paid the stud fee with relish. Apparently 'stud' comes from the same root as 'stand' and Bugler did stand – on two legs. The labourer is worthy of his hire and I will always bark well of him. Nevertheless, all I got was one biscuit.

After my bridegroom had been driven away, with more than his tail between his legs, the Boss and the Chap were more flaked out than I was and, after a diary note had been inserted with D (for delivery) Day being calculated as 2 March, we all flopped for half an hour. There had been no need for him to carry me over the threshold as we were already at home, not that he would have risked another hernia by doing so.

Suddenly, the village church bells started to ring out joyfully. It was for someone else's wedding but it was a happy coincidence. We consulted our special friend, Elsie, the verger, at the church next door, and she assured us that when the bells rang out for the New Year on the following day she would see to it that they would also be ringing for me. She's a good friend. As for a wedding cake, the nearest thing was a piece of the Christmas cake but at least I got that.

When the Boss had recovered from her exertions she celebrated by going out to the sales in Newbury and, as soon as her back was turned, the Chap gave me an extra big meal, partly as a reward for making such a good try, but also because, hopefully I was eating for at least seven – his ideal number – and perhaps ten. Suddenly he was even more solicitous than usual – with me in my condition! Later that evening the Boss drank to me and the potential pups with champagne. Being teetotal, the Chap had some fruit juice while they fantasized by counting the pups before there was any certainty that they had been conceived. They were also wondering whether I would have enough teats to feed them all. I have only nine.

On 28 January, just four weeks after my devirgination, if there is such a word, I was taken to the vet for the moment of truth. Knowing that I would begin to shake as soon as I realized where I was they kept me in the car until the vet was ready for me. I was smartly whipped in but started to shake, nevertheless, while the vet fiddled around my abdomen, pressing here and pressing there which I did not like at all. I thought the Chap was going to throw his hat in the air when the vet announced, 'I can feel at least four, so she's pregnant all right!' So it was official. I was a bitch in waiting. Being four weeks gone I had another five to go. My immediate view was, Well, they got me into this mess so they'd better see me through it. I was sure they would. The whole pack, including the grandchildren would rally round and give me support.

On the way back, with the Boss driving, the Chap insisted on extra care when we went over the bumps of the village level crossing in the car. Thank goodness I hadn't let them down. And neither had Bugler. The Chap rang Bugler's mistress that night with the good news that I was definitely 'in the pudding club', which sounded promising for me, though I didn't get any. The lady was delighted and so, according to her, was Bugler who wagged his tail and, no doubt, like the males of another species with which I am familiar, thought it was all down to him.

The Boss wrote to her friend the Duke of Fife, advising him that it looked as though his long-awaited pup was in the bag, which was just where it should be at that stage. She also wrote to Shirley Deterding, a well-known Norfolk shooting-and-fishing lady, who wanted a chocolate pup.

There were extra recompenses, apart from the sudden onset of super-solicitude. The Boss knew that I would be eating for at least five (including myself) and possibly ten, so my daily beaten-up egg in milk, which I had been getting on spec, was guaranteed. Indeed, there was one morning when the Boss told the Chap, to my great satisfaction, 'You can't have an egg for your breakfast this morning because there's only one and it's for Dido.' She had her priorities right at last. Bitches and prospective children first! With each egg my smile became more seraphic. I also got extra bones to provide the pups with plenty of calcium, though I must confess that I did not have them in mind when I was gnawing them.

There was some argument as to whether I was looking 'radiant', as pregnant women are alleged to do. But how can you look radiant when completely covered with a chocolate fur coat? The Boss was nearer the mark when she said that I looked 'questioning' as though saying, 'You got me into this mess.'

The good news meant that the Chap and I could also press ahead with our next book in some certainty that we could call it *A Box of Chocolates*, though four pups would hardly be enough to justify that title. The Chap told me it just had to be at least six and, preferably, seven.

With so many people knowing that I was 'in a certain condition', as they used to say in less brutal times, it was hardly a secret I could hug to myself as recent virgins are supposed to do. The fact that I was 'expecting' was soon all over the village, where there was widespread rejoicing with people giving me an extra pat when we went to the post-box.

While morning sickness is not unknown in dogs I didn't have it, but the Chap would nod, sagely, on the odd mornings when I was off my breakfast, though I generally ate it up later. He also seemed convinced that all was well when instead of announcing that he was taking me for a walk he would say, 'I'm taking her for a waddle.' Not very complimentary but reassuring. However, as I was not getting quite as fat in the right places as might be expected, the Chap sometimes wondered whether it was wind after all, as he crudely put it. Was I being stuffed with extra food to no useful purpose? Well, I certainly was not going to complain. All we could do was to carry on and await the moment of truth when he promised that if it was wind I would be going on the crashiest of all crash diets.

As for myself, one day I felt sure that I was in pup: the next I was not so sure because the remarks I heard were so confusing. One evening the Boss would be certain that she could feel little heartbeats and see flutterings: in the morning she would be equally sure that there was nothing there. Every night when the Chap bedded me down, he prodded me gently to see if he could feel any pups and usually seemed convinced that he could feel one, which he called Buster, assuring me that in every litter there was always one, usually a male, with a big head. I had no option but to take his word for it, but did not feel it was a very nice name for one of my sons. Nor did I take it kindly when he started to call me Fatty and Pudding, having been instrumental in getting me into that shape. It was true, though, my figure was going to the sports and I was finding it less easy to trip upstairs so blithely, carrying perhaps ten puppies inside me. Otherwise, I just felt the same. Humans say, 'Laugh and grow fat.' 'Grow fat and laugh,' I say. In view of all the services I render, there has to be some reward!

On a day when the Chap was reasonably convinced that puppies were on the way he set about making me a whelping box of solid oak which was only fitting, even if it had once been a bookcase. He's quite useful with tools – what I call a good pawyman. The sides were high enough to prevent baby pups from climbing out, but easy for me to negotiate. He cleverly fitted it with slats to prevent cot deaths because it is easy to lie on a pup and squash it, which was a horrible thought. He made it down in the cellar while I stood at the top watching him sawing and hammering away and cursing when anything went wrong or he hit his thumb. There was no way I was going down those steps to have to climb them again in my condition. He was so keen that I wouldn't have been surprised if my lying-in bed had ended up as a four poster. The Boss moved all her precious plants out of the small conservatory, where they wanted me to pup, putting them in various rooms. Softly, softly catchee Dido was the plan for getting me there. First they put my kitchen beanbag, on which I usually sleep, into the warm conservatory. A few nights later this was replaced by the whelping box with the bag in it. Then the bag was removed and all I was left with was the box with a lot of torn-up newspaper in it.

I went along with this pantomime to please them but I had no intention of whelping in any box if I

41

could help it. Whelping is something for which any self-respecting bitch needs absolute privacy and darkness and I had already dug a deep hole in a dry place in the garden – a den like my old ancestor, the wolf bitch, dug and still digs – where I could retreat when my time came. Clearly, there was going to be a battle of wits as well as wills.

I continued to dig, nipping out into the garden at night from the conservatory, and the Chap cursed me every time he shovelled the earth back but, knowing that I would dig it out again that night, he always took my collar off so that I wouldn't get caught up in branches or the trellis work.

My photographer friend from the *Daily Mail*, Mike Hollist, was alerted and promised to come down to photograph me with my brood – a picture destined for the front page, no doubt.

When we got within a week or so of my expected delivery date, the Chap cut the lawn in preparation for putting up a run for the pups when the weather was nice. Being winter it hadn't been looked at by them for some time, though, of course, I make use of it every morning before they get up. He grumbled because it took him so long to remove my accumulated offerings but if you have to eat for a possible ten then you do the consequences for ten as well. Why couldn't he see that?

Some doubt continued right up to within a few days. The Chap thought it could still be a phantom as there was no sign of any milk. 'Do you think that if I stuck a pin in her belly it would collapse?' he asked the Boss. She couldn't understand why I was still able to bounce around on my stomach with my back legs splayed or to lie on my back luxuriously on the bed – my 'dying swan act', as she called it, though, typically the Chap preferred 'dying duck'.

When we got near the sixty-third day they began to refuse invitations to dinner because I couldn't be left alone in case I went into labour, though day by day, doubts about my condition had continued to grow. When there was still no sign of any milk the Chap declared, 'We'll give her another couple of days. They are not always on time. Then she's for the vet!'

The vet it was. After rubbing his hand up and down my belly he announced that there was nothing there and admitted, rather ruefully, that either he must have misdiagnosed or I had reabsorbed the embryos, which sometimes happens. He said I had experienced a phantom pregnancy. Some phantom! Having eaten for ten I looked like a porpoise. But then, given a chance, any Labrador worthy of the name would eat for twenty. So I had sacrificed my virginity to no purpose – that is, apart from the grub.

For a moment I had high hopes when the Chap said something about my goose being cooked. But I got his meaning when he couldn't resist telling the Boss that all those yolks had been on her, as, indeed, had been the whites.

So there it was – an absolute dogastrophe! What the Chap called the biggest fraud ever inflicted by dog on man. From being a radiant mother-to-be I was suddenly reduced to being a fat slob committed to a strict diet, eating for one, and sparingly at that. It had been the Boss's fault that I had become hooked on eggs – I still get the urge whenever I hear one being broken – but I got the cold-turkey treatment, no eggs at all which, of course, subjected me to withdrawal symptoms. Suddenly eating for one is tough.

There is no more justice in the canine world than in the human. I had done my stuff and gone through all the right motions. It hadn't been my fault that I had been eating for ten. Nor was it my fault that the vet had got it wrong and the rest of the pack had deluded themselves. They had been more expectant than I was – a sight more, as it turned out.

While the Chap was concerned about losing face in the village, and with all the friends who had been ringing up, all I was worried about was losing my extra rations. Someone suggested that we should hire a litter of chocolate pups – they are often advertised in doggy papers – and pass them off as mine, but this was quickly rejected for ethical reasons. The Chap had been deeply involved in the famous case in which 'being economical with the truth' had been equated with lying, and wanted no more of it. Anyway, the pedigree forms would have given the game away. So, instead, the Boss had to write to the Duke of Fife and the others who had been promised pups. The local paper and my photographer friend, Mike Hollist, had to be given the sad news. So had Bugler and his mistress, who were deeply disappointed. The Editor of the *Newbury Weekly News*, no less, made an announcement in his column, describing me as the 'chocolate temptress', so I must be famous when I get my picture in the paper even when I don't do anything! Fans, including journalists, wrote or telephoned with their sympathy.

On being consulted again the vet said that, though I would be just five by the time my next heat was due, I would not be too old to have a litter. He thought that I might be one of those bitches that ovulates early and, therefore, had been taken to Bugler too late. So, before being taken to him again I should be given a blood test that would show whether I was about to ovulate or not. I didn't fancy that but it was too far away to worry about it.

After a couple of days of gloom, with the great whelping box being stacked away, the torn-up paper consigned to the bin and the plants returned to the conservatory – except for the precious Streptocarpus which had been killed by frost in an outhouse – the Chap accepted the anticlimax. 'OK,' he said, 'we'll write it off as a dress rehearsal.'

So there I was, still a miss after all – a near-miss – but a miss, nevertheless, faced with the problems of sex and the single bitch. But, at least, the episode had livened up the scene which can be dull in winter.

3 All's Super that Ends Super

Only a mother knows a mother's fondness

In the country, June is the traditional wedding month, but I held out until July. Charmed-life Charlie was on cue again, taking up his vigil outside the back gate three days before there were signs observable to humans that I was in season. I thought that he was looking rather old and this time I did not fancy being a toy-girl for an old roué. Toy-dog used to mean something different, but now, like gay dog, it has been given a sleazy implication in your sex-ridden society. My views were academic, though, because, now that I was a star, precautions against unwelcome suitors had to be especially secure. The Chap was taking no chances this time, all aspects of modern technology being pressed into my service. On the third day of my heat I was taken to the vet whose practice had moved to posh new premises in Donnington, a nearby village where there is a castle which, as usual, was bashed about by Cromwell. Nevertheless, brand-new or not, the moment I went through the swing-door I recognized it for what it was and immediately got a fit of the shivers.

I was given a general check-up by my personal vet, Julian, who is a nice, gentle man with a good beanbag-side manner, though still a vet. He gave me a vaginal swab to see if I had any infections. I didn't. Then, on the eighth day, I was taken back again for a blood test so that my hormones could be examined to see when I was due to ovulate. I didn't like that at all because Julian had to shave a little patch of hair off my leg and then stuck a needle into a vein. A pretty nurse came to help in holding my leg and, though it did not hurt, the whole set-up made my teeth chatter. That afternoon, Julian telephoned with the result – I wasn't ready and would have to undergo the whole ordeal again two days later.

Concerned that I might be going off the boil, because for twenty-four hours it looked as though Charlie had lost interest, the Chap risked taking me for a walk to the post-box and round the village, but all I met was a couple of canine eunuchs who could not have cared less. What a dreadful thing to do to a dog, I always think.

Well, off we went again to the vet for the second blood test, which was every bit as traumatic for me as the first, and again came the telephone call, 'She's still not ready yet. Come again in two more days.' Julian explained that, while all seemed to be going well, I was obviously a 'late ovulator' which, he now thought, explained why I had not conceived in my previous encounter.

While all this was going on, the Chap took me down to the river to fish and walked me on the Common when there was nobody else about. I left plenty of visiting-cards and, no doubt, set lots of the local dogs alight. The thought of it put extra zest in my post-poop shuffle and the Chap noted that I had never flung grass, earth and stones so far.

Two days later, with Charlie and another bigger dog back on station, I went for my third test. Will I have any blood left if they go on like this? I thought. I shivered and chattered more than ever. This time Julian telephoned to say that I would definitely be ovulating within forty-eight hours. His advice was that I should be taken to Bugler boy the following morning, a Saturday, and then again on the Monday morning. The Chap brought the news to me by singing a ditty – 'You're getting married in the morning, Ding dog the bells are going to chime . . .' The rest, which had something about 'a whopper' in it, was too rude for me to repeat here but, at least, we knew where we were going. The Chap telephoned Bugler's mistress and he was ready and available. I don't know who had been getting more frustrated, me or the rest of the pack. Anything to get rid of that blood-test trauma!

It was beautiful, full-summer weather for my second wedding day. So off we went, just the Chap and me, to Bugler's home at Greatworth Manor. The bride was wearing chocolate, as before, enhanced, of course, by my best buttercup-yellow collar.

Sure enough, Charlie was at the gate as we left, indicating that he was ready to save us all that long journey. I looked at him out of the back window as we sped up the street. He started to bark, obviously aware that he was being thwarted, and followed us all the way down to the level crossing, taking his life in his legs again. The morning traffic was heavy and, as usual, the Chap marvelled at the way Charlie survived, though it was all very complimentary to me. He seemed to know what was going to happen to me and resented it. Cheesed-off Charlie would have been a better name for him at that moment.

Of course, this time I was not a virgin but, if I liked, I could pretend to be, like a lot of women do, though little more store is set by virginity in your world than in ours these days.

I staggered the Chap by making it clear that I knew where we were when we got within a mile of Bugler's home. I stood up in the back of the car and started whimpering in the way I do when I am excited by anticipation. As we drove into the grounds of Greatworth Manor Bugler was waiting for me. I hadn't seen him for six months and he looked more handsome than ever. He was also raring to go because he had been short of wives for a while and not flaked out by shooting.

He sounded the charge again immediately and we chased each other round and round the garden until he began to pant. I was not going to be had lightly and it was good for him to get a few ritual rebuffs. In fact, after twenty minutes in the hot sun, he was puffing so much that the Chap feared he would run out of steam. So his mistress had a great idea – she would take us all inside into the cool sitting room of the old stone house where we couldn't run about like lunatics. Sue left us to make the Chap a coffee and the Chap was looking so miserable that I thought it only fair to let him have his coffee in peace. So I stood still and let Bugler get on with it. Suddenly we were knotted again – this time for about fifteen minutes – and when Mrs Towers-Clark returned she was delighted, saying that she reckoned on one pup for every minute we stayed knotted. Fifteen pups! That would be ridiculous!

Anyway, it was emission accomplished again and, once we were released, Bugler was very affectionate to me, as I was to him. We took off for home straight away to give the good news to the Boss who had been unable to accompany us. When the Chap opened his sandwich lunch on the drive back, there was a Bonio biscuit for me. Bless her!

The Boss was delighted with the news, as were the village neighbours. Even Charlie, who was back on station, seemed to have forgiven me or, at any rate, decided to cut his losses. That night we gave a dinner party attended by my Uncle Marcus and Auntie Lily Sieff. The following morning, the Boss went to church and said a little prayer. The Chap, who took me fishing, put his faith in Bugler and wrote in his diary for 26 September – exactly nine weeks later – 'Dido due to pup'.

I recovered my strength during the rest of Sunday and on Monday morning the Boss accompanied us back to see Bugler for a repeat performance. Oh dear! I'm afraid I disgraced myself again. We were delighted to see each other and did our mad runs round the garden but I was not to be had again either outside or inside the house. Even though it would have amounted to rape, the Chap tried holding me by the collar but I just collapsed and made things impossible. They tried holding me over a bale of hay but, gallantly perhaps, Bugler did not like that.

The Chap was displeased as every trick failed. He does not like being thwarted and ignored me completely on the way back, though the Boss, being a woman, was more understanding. All they could do was to put their faith in the first mating, the Boss being so confident that she calculated that 26 September would be perfectly timed for just a week after our return from our autumn salmon-fishing holiday in Scotland. Clever little me! The Chap has lost a few salmon through faulty knots which he had tied himself. Now his literary future – and mine – depended on the efficacy of one dog-knot.

I was momentarily perturbed when they called at the vet's place as they passed it on the way back from the abortive mating, but it was only to report the situation to Julian. Dear old ever-hopeful Charlie appeared, as though by magic, within a few minutes of my return home and when our noses met under the locked back gate the Chap said he was probably saying, 'See, you should have had me, after all. You wouldn't have got away from me, small as I am.'

The vet suggested that he might give me an ultrasonic scan in twenty-nine days which would show if I was carrying any pups, but the Boss decided against it arguing, quite rightly, that the trauma would not be good for me and it was not worth that just to satisfy the Chap's curiosity. Within two days even Charlie had lost all interest and we were able to resume our normal walks not caring whether we met any dogs or not.

By the thirty-fourth day the Chap and the Boss were in such a stew with doubt that they changed their minds and asked the vet to come and see me. It was Julian and he deliberately left his bag in his car so that I would not smell the equipment. I have to admit that, without his white coat, I did not recognize him at first but, once he began to get really familiar and prod around, I began to suspect that I had been diddled. Luckily, the examination did not last long and to the Chap's surprise, if not astonishment, I was pronounced pregnant. Julian said he was prepared to bet a bottle of whisky on it but the Chap said he would reserve judgement. It's sad, how little faith some people have.

There was some welcome talk about increasing my food ration, starting with the eggs in milk again, but, otherwise, Julian prescribed a normal life, assuring us that I would take it all in my stride, which took the bark right out of my mouth. When the Boss returned from her shopping, expecting another let-down, she was delighted, feeling that a new chapter in our lives – the one I am dictating now – was about to open. She celebrated with a stiff Scotch and I got a slice of Death by Chocolate, a marvellous concoction made at the Bistro up the road, which the Boss had been holding back in the fridge for such an occasion.

The news meant that I would be rather advanced in my pregnancy when we went for our Scottish holiday in mid-September, but we decided to take Julian's advice and continue as normal. The Chap called the trip my maternity leave but he was determined to go salmon fishing there anyway.

I had a glorious time on the Tay river, at Kinnaird, just mooching about while the Chap and the Boss fished away up to their waists in water. I spent lots of it myself standing as deep as I could because it took the weight off my expanding belly, with the water exerting a welcome upthrust according to a principle which, the Chap explained, had been discovered by some old Greek codger called Archimedes. We didn't catch many fish even though the Chap was wearing his Dido pullover for luck – to the surprise and amusement of the gillies.

A famous gynaecologist and obstetrician, an old friend whom we call Goldfinger, was there fishing as well so I felt secure. He palpated me a few times and raised doubts in the Chap's mind by saying that he couldn't feel anything, but all the guests agreed that I was 'well in the club' and that this was the phantom to end all phantoms if that is what it was. I was also interviewed and photographed on the river for the *Scottish Field* which should extend my fame in the country which, like the rest of my pack, I have come to love so much.

As I was getting so fat we cut short our holiday by one day to get me home in good time. A pity really, for I still had a week to go. Anyway, there I was again, having to eat for up to ten with eggs whipped up in milk and two meals a day instead of one. What a sacrifice! The things I do for literature! The Chap, too made his extra contribution, remarking, when clearing the lawn prior to mowing it – 'She's not only *eating* for ten!'

Pregnant females are supposed to have strange fads about foods but I just wanted more of everything. There was one occasion, though, when the Boss was walking me on Hungerford Common and I disturbed a fieldmouse from a tuft of grass. I ran after it, seized it and the Boss, thinking I was just playing a dog-and-mouse game, was amazed to see its tail disappearing down my throat. I had swallowed it like an oyster, and I don't really know why because I had never eaten one before, regarding mice, with some disdain, as cat food. Perhaps it was a throwback to my ancestry because wolves will eat mice when they feel really famished, as a pregnant dog always does, I assure you.

In the days thereafter, I was closely inspected every morning, with hopes mounting as my rib-cage widened and my normally tiny nipples enlarged. In the evenings, when I was stretched out in the living room, the Boss spent more time looking for movements of my puppies than watching the television screen. It was the Chap who spotted them first. While he was comforting me with his hand on my side, four days before I was due, he felt great bumpings going on inside me. Not even I, with all my magical powers, could create a phantom simulating a litter of pups moving about. So, at last, he was convinced and the new fear, with so much commotion going on, was that I might have too many!

I wonder what pups are up to when they bounce about inside the womb. Are they wagging their tails, like human embryos suck their thumbs? They seemed to be doing everything else. However, I found a way of quietening them down. One of my party tricks is to lie on my belly with my legs splayed out flat and to bounce forwards like a seal. I could still do it even when my belly was enormous and it shut the pups up, smartly.

The Boss began to wonder how many might be chocolate dogs and how many bitches. Typically, the Chap said he was wondering how many might be Jack Russells!

Up from the cellar came the great oak whelping box, which the Chap, bless him, decided to extend by six inches, a formidable job, so that I could lay my full length in it. They put it into the conservatory which, since it can be heated, was to serve as a nursery for pups instead of plants, and immediately got up to all their old tricks to get me to accept it and forget the nice holes I had dug in a dry part of the garden. One of them was putting into the box the little, old, brown beanbag which my first mistress, Alison, had left when she had parted with me, my big blue one being far too large for that purpose. They also put in plenty of newspaper so that I could tear it up and make a nest with it if I felt like it.

Each night my dog doors were shut to keep me out of the garden and the Boss, who was getting broodier by the day, slept with one ear open in case I began to give birth in the night. The brown beanbag was removed and left outside the big box with only the newspaper left for me to lie on.

Big as I was I had to be exercised and at some stage of the day the Chap, being desperate for a few casts, would ask the Boss, 'Do you think it's safe to take the porpoise down to the river for a bit?' There would be a brief inspection and down we went – until the day before the Chap's diary said 'Dido due to pup!' when the Boss thought it was tempting fate too much.

I began to pant late on the Friday evening and, during that night, the Boss and the Chap came down every two hours to see how I was faring. At the 6 a.m. visit I wasn't to be seen at all and the Boss found me behind one of the curtains hung up to darken the conservatory to make it more like a natural den. I had diddled them after all and produced my first baby – a strong chocolate dog, Son of Dido – on the lino. It was because he was squeaking away so lustily that the Boss knew where I was. She could not get me into the whelping box but I did deign to go on to the old flat brown beanbag which had been my bed when I had been a pup myself. I decided to stay on it and produced the rest of my litter there.

By that time it was 7 a.m. and the Boss and the Chap were watching through the glass kitchen door. On the chance that I might not pup until the Sunday the Chap had left a local morning appointment of some importance in his diary but had to ring up and cancel it, explaining hurriedly, 'Sorry! My dog's gone into labour.' I wonder what they really thought at the other end.

As each pup was born the Boss made sure that its face was free of membrane so that it could breathe. I was only surprised that she and the Chap were not wearing masks and gowns! If anything, I had a surfeit of midwives but it was just as well. My fifth pup, a girl, was a long time coming and was not breathing when she did. The Boss, bless her, knew just what to do, holding her and shaking her gently until her lungs and nose were free of mucus and she could breathe easily. I then gave the pup special attention, licking her hard which soon had her nosing about looking for milk. By that time, the Boss and I had reached such a rapport that when the next pups began to emerge she kept saying, 'Push, Dido!' I got the hang of it and did not wince nor bark aloud.

By that time, the Chap had retired to his study, with the door open so that he could hear everything. It was just as well because it was woman's (and bitch's) work. I was getting exhausted and was grateful when the Boss offered me a bowl of water which I would not have been able to reach. I drank deep and long and had never enjoyed a drink so much.

My last pup, number seven, was born at 1 p.m. so I had not only presented them with exactly the number they preferred but right on the button as regards the expected day. By happy coincidence I was one of seven puppies myself so, maybe, one of mine is the seventh pup of a seventh pup and there should be something specially magical about that.

The pack had been increased to ten, with five dogs and two Mark-2 Didos, and not a runt among them, which was proof enough of Bugler's doghood. All were soon squeaking lustily – a lovely noise which was music to the human ears as much as to mine, especially as it brought back memories of their previous litters of Spaniels and Ridgebacks, all from much-loved bitches. They would have liked more females but we all have to take what we get. As it is the male who controls the sex of the offspring it was certainly not my responsibility. It is, literally, in the lap of the dogs.

By the time my labour was completed the sun was shining warmly so the Boss enticed me out into the garden with some food while the Chap smartly transferred the puppies into the failed whelping box because they were moving about so strongly that they had to be contained, especially on the future occasions when I would need to stretch my legs. So the old fellow won that one in the end.

With the mission finally accomplished, the Boss got the sherry out and our daily help, Janet, who is an old treasured friend of us all, joined in the celebration of the happy event. Being a non-drinker, the Chap celebrated with a coffee and a doughnut. I think that they were as exhausted as I was, though I summoned up enough energy to consume my usual share of the doughnut.

Of course, there was relief all round that all the pups were chocolate, exactly like their mum and dad. I had clinched the title for this book. We telephoned Julian, the vet, to give him the score and thank him for his earlier endeavours. Then we rang Bugler's mistress, Sue Towers-Clark, to give her and Bugler the good news. For the neighbours a bulletin was posted on the back gate, underneath my photograph which warns people to keep out –

> *26 September. Dido has been safely delivered of seven puppies. Mother and babies (all chocolate) are doing well.*

I did not want to do much but sleep and lick my brood. Now that it was over I was feeling totally relaxed. I know that I would have felt terrible if I had disappointed the Chap and the Boss – and myself – a second time. My box of chocolates would have remained a bone-dream and Charmed-life Charlie would have had the last laugh. A lot of famous female authors have been old maids. I am glad that I am not one of them.

4 My Magnificent Seven

Who dost they seven-fold gifts impart

The Chap says that in the human world seven is a magic number. The sudden appearance of seven fat, chocolate roly-polies was magic to me, and looking at them in their box I could see another meaning to the term 'pudding club', of which people had been assuring me for weeks that I was a member. News of their arrival spread so fast that fans were soon ringing up with messages of congratulations. On that very first evening a doctor telephoned from the wilds of Buckingham wanting a chocolate bitch and arranging to come and see us all in a fortnight. Treats were pushed through the letter-box and 'Get well' cards came in the post, though there was nothing wrong with me. In fact, following the human trend, I was encouraged to be on the move as quickly as possible. I required no encouragement to get out into the garden because I needed to dig. While the Chap was furious, as usual, at least he understood why I was doing it. The wolf, and no doubt the wild dog too, moves her cubs to different dens from time to time to reduce the chance of discovery by predators, and, of course, dens, which do not make themselves, have to be ready to receive them. The fear and the knowledge were still in my genes and had to be dealt with however much I might trust the rest of the pack to make sure that my pups would never be threatened. Because my minders feared that I might carry the pups out to one of my holes in the night they locked the dog flaps. This meant that by the early morning I was bursting to get out, but one of them, usually the Boss, was down by 6 a.m. to open the door.

Almost from birth the pups could crawl about on their bellies and each day they gathered strength, which was soon great enough to lift their heads off the floor of the box. As they were not only blind but completely deaf I did not waste any breath calling to them but there was no doubt that their senses of smell and touch were working by the ease with which each of them found its way to a nipple. As newly born pups are not warm-blooded, because their thermostats are not properly developed, I had to do all I could to cuddle them up and make sure that none of them could crawl away on a chilly day and develop hypothermia. Of course, being in the big box greatly reduced this danger and the conservatory was fitted with a heater which automatically switched on when the temperature dropped. The only risk was from a long power-cut in the small hours and, though this happened once, it was a warm night. When the pups were asleep and I was taking a breather from them they reduced the hypothermia risk by spending most of their time in a heap.

On the third day I was taken for my usual short walk round the allotments and then, gradually, the distance was extended until we were soon back on the old routine. I thought it was unkind of the Chap to call me Baggy when my teats were doing such a great job.

Sadly the trout season had ended on 30 September so I could not be taken to our stretch of the river. Of course, the Chap had fished on to the last day and, without me there to look after him, he had tripped over a rabbit hole and came back limping. My own leg had become very stiff through lying in the whelping box and the Boss had a trapped nerve so we made a rather ridiculous sight, the whole pack limping in unison as we toddled up to the village shops. Still, it paid off because the Boss went into the town to buy me a foam rubber base to the whelping box which ended my stiffness.

Normally a walk in a village could be taken without concern but, on the day that I was safely confined and giving birth, an extraordinary event had taken place outside the village store, which is also the newspaper shop. A man who has a nice Afghan hound, tied it to a post not six feet from the shop door and went in for his newspaper. When he emerged he saw two young thugs trying to lift the dog into the boot of their car. He laid into one of them with his stick and they dropped the dog and made off. Dog-napping has become all too common in our area, where the victims are being sold for some purpose or other, but for it to happen so blatantly on a busy corner of a little village was frightening. Fortunately, the Chap always has his knobbly blackthorn thumbstick with him and would be only too keen to use it should anyone try to dognap me.

My happy event was quickly reported in the *Newbury Weekly News*, which was only fair considering that they had headlined my picture, 'The chocolate temptress' after my phantom. From the publicity point of view I could not have timed my litter more brilliantly to coincide with the emergence of the paperback of *One Dog and Her Man*. It was scheduled to appear on 22

60

October when the pups should be at their most photo-genic, having been partially weaned, though still keen to take my milk, so I could leave them for a short time should a photo-opportunity demand it.

My first interview was with Pauline Peters of the *Evening Standard*, which serves all London. As it was only the eleventh day since my confinement the pups were not ready to be photographed. In fact, though they were trying to stand, they could barely manage it and kept falling over. So it was agreed that the photographer would have to come down a few days later when they were at least a fortnight old, by which time they should be trying to walk. He took scores of pictures. The result, which appeared on Fireworks Day, was quite splendid – a whole page of the paper devoted to me and with a large picture of me, the Chap and one of my babies.

We did some nice radio programmes, but the highlight was a lovely feature on Central Television organized by a friend of mine called Robin Powell who brought a team to our house. I was starred, directing operations with my Chap on the next book, playing with my pups and larking about down on the river. We made a video recording and often show it to visitors, along with the one showing me opening my bank account.

There were times when my walks were for ulterior motives of which I was unaware, such as the occasion when Julian, the vet, came to amputate the puppies' dew-claws. It was just as well that I was removed from the scene because I would have fought for them tooth and claw, including dew-claw, because I still have mine. As some of my pups could well end up as gun dogs, Julian recommended their removal because he sees so many painful cases where they have been accidentally torn away. I agreed that his intentions were honourable and forgave him completely when, on examining me after my return, he suggested that my food should be increased still further to double the normal quantity, with lots of milk to supply the calcium of which my pups were depriving me. He thought that within a week or so I would be unable to eat enough for my metabolism to compensate for all that the pups would be taking from me. What a challenge for any Labrador and especially for this one! As the Chap frequently says when he has made some effort which he considers Herculean, 'There has to be some reward', and the extra grub was it. Needless to say I beat the challenge with no trouble at all and did my puppies proud, as well as myself.

Really, though, the pups were reward enough in themselves and I have never looked so content as when lying in the great box with my pups all in a row sucking away. It was already clear that the pups were a credit to both me and to Bugler. We had both put our stamp on them. By keeping his study door open the Chap could hear them squeaking in the nursery so he didn't feel lonely and could easily get to me if anything sounded wrong. It rarely did. The squeaks were usually of anticipation and the creaks were of contentment – what the Chap called the 'bellyful bleat'. Though the Chap prides himself on being observant, it was the Boss who was first to notice that, when I got into the box to feed the pups, I usually alternated the side on which I lay down so that the right side set of teats were on top for one feed and the left side on top for the next. (Frankly, I hadn't noticed it myself.)

Soon they all developed that very particular puppy smell which the Chap says should be incorporated into an after-shave perfume for men because it sends all females broody. Though they looked more or less alike, differing only slightly in size, they soon displayed their own little ways, each being a unique creation, and it was not long before a peck-order was established. As the Chap had predicted, Buster, my first born, was soon top dog, but with nine teats for seven pups nobody had to wait so nobody was badly pup-pecked.

The Chap and the Boss chose chocolate names for them all except Buster – Mars Bar for the lightest coloured; Bourneville for the darkest; Walnut Whip for one which had a whirl in his fur; Yorkie; Rolo and Wispa. There was not one light enough to be called Truffle. They soon began to look different and I could see exactly what some of them would look like when they grew up, the pup being father of the dog.

The Chap and the Boss could do whatever they wished with my pups because my trust in them was total and it was essential that they should all be handled regularly to socialize them and prepare them for life in a human pack. Otherwise a puppy can turn into a dog that is withdrawn and lacking in affection for its human owners and that would never do for one of mine. A pup needs to be able to form ties with both humans and other dogs. Mine soon did and quickly came to recognize the Chap and the Boss, licking them when they were picked up.

I would not let anyone else approach the pups un-challenged, surprising myself with the determination of my protectiveness. On the fourteenth day the first eyes were open – just slits at first. They were light blue because, according to 'Know-all', the pigment had not yet developed in their irises and the blue colour was the muscles showing through. (Trust him to be unromantic, though, being colour blind as all we dogs are, it meant nothing to me.) Their ear canals had also opened, which made my life a lot more difficult because the sound of only one pup sucking quickly aroused the rest even if they were asleep.

It was also on the fourteenth day that I heard the first growl and the first little bark – a great moment in a dog's life. The Chap said that they were quite precocious, though never having had pups before I could not judge. On the sixteenth day I observed the first boxing match between two of my boys. Soon there was ear-pulling all round and I had some difficulty in convincing them that dog does not eat dog. My real problem came when they were about three weeks old and their sharp little teeth began to come through the gums. They were so rough with me that I began to feel really sore and learned the wisdom of the adage let sleeping pups lie! It was a great relief when the Boss decided that it was time they were weaned and could start to eat for themselves. She and the Chap were specially affectionate when the puppies were giving me a hard time, which I appreciated very much. There is another adage that you can take a pup to the milk but you can't make him drink, but all mine lapped away at their first dish of Lactol with no trouble at all. I didn't witness this milestone in their lives because it was done while I was taken out in the car but I quickly noticed the reduced demand and was grateful for the Boss's efforts to take the burden off my titties.

Within two days they were taking solid puppy food mixed first with Lactol, then just with water. This was not their first experience of solid food because I had regurgitated some of mine for them, which was quite a little sacrifice, though it was easier for me in the long run when they took it directly rather than as milk. Soon they were eating dry food, but it did have meat in it so I enjoyed cleaning up what they left, though they soon learned to clean up every scrap. They grew really rapidly and recognized water as something that they must drink regularly without being taught by me. By that time they had learned to wag their tails and they made a delightful picture all in a row, or sometimes in a circle, at seven bowls. A big single bowl caused less work but the rapacious Buster liked standing with all four legs in the dish – a real pup in the manger.

The whelping box was taken away and the pups had the whole conservatory as a playground. Their curiosity, a sure sign that their brains were developing, drove them to explore everything around them and they were soon up to mischief, learning every trick in the book and a few new ones as they went. I had great fun playing with them but there were limits to the liberties I was prepared to condone, teaching them a thing or two in the process, sometimes the hard way. The Chap and the Boss, too, rolled around with them with more patience than I had on the principle that, 'There is nothing like the young to keep you young.' I suppose I did it when I was a pup. The commotion in the 'dorm', after lights out, was quite something but it was remarkable how quickly the whole litter would suddenly collapse after a great burst of energy and sleep it off. They were given two plastic tubs to sleep in but they all preferred to pile into one – usually the smaller one! They did not do that for warmth, because the conservatory was kept at 70 degrees, but for the comfort of contact – the pack's knowledge that there is safety in numbers expressing itself.

By the fourth week they were establishing a bite-order though to some extent that had already been done at the teats. On sunny days they had also been introduced to an outside wired-in run – their first discovery of open space. They also started playing with their first toys, chasing golf balls about, though they had already learned to have fun tearing up paper.

Without any encouragement I had developed the habit of leaving the pups as soon as they were asleep, sometimes resting on my big beanbag and keeping an eye on them or, better still, being taken for a walk. They spent a lot of time asleep, for which I was grateful. So long as I knew that they were safe in the conservatory or in the wire cage outside, it was a relief to be away from them, especially as they were getting really boisterous, growling and barking and even fighting. I call the wire-run a cage because there had to be a roof on it to keep out the sparrow-hawk which patrols our garden every day. It can easily kill a rabbit and could certainly badly injure a puppy.

When the sun came out the pups were allowed to run free in the garden, exploring every cranny, usually under my supervision which gave me the greatest pleasure. It was fascinating to see how excited they were when they found one of my bones on the lawn, all clustering round as though they knew what a major contribution these objects, which they had never seen before, would eventually make to their lives. The Chap tested their reaction to a handful of sterilized bone-meal and their excitement suggested that some knowledge of what bones are is inherited in the genes. He also quickly spotted that some of my pups had obviously inherited my ability to excavate holes in his flower beds – what he called a new generation of 'dirty diggers'. If a day without a dog is a day without sunshine then a day with seven pups is a day without repose.

Because the nights were getting colder, they still slept in the conservatory. In the morning the Chap said that it was like mucking out seven ponies, for that was his first task. I believe that in the whole of his life he had never changed a nappy, that being woman's work in his youth, but, suddenly, he became curious about puppy excrement, ensuring that there was no abnormality that might bode ill. He received a dreadful fright one morning when the smallest of my sons, who had been off his food for a few hours, projected a continuing stream of bright-pink fluid from the wrong place. Thinking that it could only be blood, the Boss rushed the puppy to the vet who was concerned until he received an urgent telephone call from the Chap, who had been left in charge of the rest of us. Racking what remains of his brains for an explanation of this extraordinary event he remembered that, on the previous day, one of the pups had emerged from a corner near the dustbin with its face covered with ash. The tray which catches the ashes from the sitting-room fire had been left on the ground and the Chap deduced that the pup had eaten a belly-full of it, the ash being pink. The vet agreed that this was probably the explanation and, instead of losing my son, as we had all feared, he was romping round with the rest by the evening. The Boss and the Chap were not romping. They were exhausted after the trauma of what became known as Ash Tuesday.

The boy who had caused all the trouble was something of a problem pup, being more demanding than the rest, but also the brightest. He was the first to find out that he could get into the house through the two dog flaps and I fear that his new owners, who chose him because he was so lively, were not fully aware what was about to hit them. They have called him Buttons and he certainly has all his on.

As I cannot stress too often, there is always a penalty to pay for every advantage in this life. Being relieved of my pups' teeth meant that my milk had to be reduced by giving me less to eat. The Boss was as kind as she could be by doing this gradually but I noticed it, especially when egg in milk was suddenly off the menu. It is said that human mothers often make some sacrifice to their babies by losing a tooth as a result of pregnancy. My sacrifice was my lovely otter tail which used to bring me such compliments. The hairs on it disappeared in such numbers that I ended up with a tail like a Whippet, but it soon began to regrow to its former glory.

Everyone wanted to photograph the pups and we had a professional to take pictures of them all in a giant golden chocolate box with a red ribbon on it. Keeping seven wrigglers in one box was quite a problem and they were rewarded for their co-operation by being given their first dog chocs, another milestone in their lives. The *Newbury Weekly News* featured the best picture which caused a great deal of comment. We had one of the colour photographs made into our Christmas cards, which were signed by me as well.

It was only right that Bugler should be in the picture and his mistress brought him over to see us all. Whether I shall ever see him again I do not know but, much as I like him, I shall not pine for him like Queen Dido did for Aeneas. Like most bitches I am a single parent but, these days, we are in the fashion. At least Bugler is registered as the father of my young (at the Kennel Club) which is more than can be said about a lot of fathers. It cost the Chap £7 a pup to register them but it was cheap at the price, only the best being good enough for them, I reckon.

The number of people who started ringing up for chocolate pups showed how popular the colour has become. A few were put off by the price – my fame had rubbed off on it – but most of those who came to see them could not resist them and the Chap and the Boss made sure that they all went to homes where they would be treasured and loved. Of course, they could not leave us until they were eight weeks old, fully capable of feeding on their own and forming bonds with their new packs.

My two girls were the first to be sold, commanding a bigger price than the boys, which is usual these days. One of them is now called Welly for romantic reasons – her owners met while working at the Wellington Hospital in London. Their sweet, young daughter, Katie, brought me a huge bone to comfort me with a note attached promising, 'I will always look after Welly.' The other is called Tarka, the same name as my mother, and will be doing a lot of travelling, as I do, for her owner moves around a lot by car. The girls were soon followed by my favourite son, a most endearing little chap (I must be careful how I use that word) with a few white hairs on the front of his chest. The Chap said it was the result of my being frightened by Charmed-life Charlie while I was pregnant. I had a feeling that whoever first came looking for a dog would be unable to resist him and I was right. They call him Rolo – the only one of the chocolate names we had chosen – and he lives near Banbury quite close to his dad, Bugler. What is more, his new Chap is a mad keen trout angler so I guess he'll be a fishing dog, like me and his North-American ancestors. He should take to the water because he was in the river with me on most of the days when I was pregnant.

The next to get a new home was Buster. A huge man called to choose a pup and the Chap said, 'I bet he picks the biggest', which he did after only a cursory look at the rest. Buster seemed to look rather superior after that but he was soon to discover that the best-laid plans of pups and men . . .

Buttons, the smallest and, in many ways, the most ebullient boy, went to a family who are now friends so

I often meet him for a romp. The other names chosen by new owners were Charlton for another boy who lives nearby; and Pincher who, to the Chap's delight, went to the head-keeper of the Clarendon shoot in Wiltshire to be a gun dog, making up, no doubt, for my deficiences. I enjoyed the keeper's joke in deciding to call him Pincher! I can just hear him shouting across the fields, 'Come in, Pincher, you . . .' We thought that, as the last pup to go, Pincher would feel very lonely on his own in the conservatory but, for most of the time, he behaved as though he had always wanted a place of his own.

The combined weight of my pups at eight weeks of age was nearly six stones, so the pack had done them proud. With Bugler's help, I had done my duty in helping not only to spread the Labrador brand of happiness but to disseminate the chocolate variety so that, one day, there will be enough of us to establish a Chocolate Labrador Society, like the one for the Yellow kind, but we are all awaiting approval from the Kennel Club.

I felt that it would have been delightful to have been left with one pup as a permanent playmate but it would have caused problems. When the Chap and the Boss go away I am usually welcome wherever we stay but two large dogs might not be. While I am also welcome to most of the fishermen down on the river, two of us might be too much. So, sadly, they all had to go and I was pupless in Gaza. The Chap took the pawprints of all of them for my album and, of course, we had lots of colour pictures for remembrance.

No doubt they all missed me and felt lonely for a while in their new homes, but not for long. Buttons whimpered only on the first night and the only time Welly whimpered was when she heard Katie practising the violin. But she soon got used to that and is now a great fan of Classic FM. Like you humans, we Labradors are an adaptable lot.

Still the partings had been bitter-sweet and it was Gloomsville at our house for a few days, in spite of the relief from all the noise and work – but not for long. Just when my couple were fully appreciating the luxury of reading the papers and letters in bed without having to get up to sort the pups out, the owners of Buster telephoned to say that they would have to dispose of him because their asthmatic baby was allergic to his fur! We wanted some control over his new owners so, with no hesitation, the Chap and the Boss bought him back and we were landed with him until we could find him a new home. I was over-joyed to see him, especially as he was big enough to romp around with me. We had rumbustious times together, starting with a roll on the couple's bed in the morning, followed by larking round the Chap's legs in his study and wild fun in the sitting room in the evening. After an astonishing burst of energy for such a little fellow, Buster would crash out into a deep sleep. We could have had intermittent fun all night but the Boss was not prepared to risk the consequences of leaving us together unsupervised for so long. So Buster had to be confined at night in the heated cage-run in the garage but proved to be such a canine Houdini that the only way to keep him in was to tie the lid down with rope. On the first night, before this was done, he escaped and ate through a live electric flex, exposing the wires in several places without being injured. How he did this has puzzled the Chap ever since.

A couple who were looking for a chocolate pup and telephoned the Kennel Club were given our number and came to see Buster. I knew that they would be unable to resist him and they couldn't. The Boss liked the look of them and felt sure that they would give my boy the affection he needed and deserved so off he went to live in a village in West Sussex. Care was taken to ensure that I could not see the going of him. Immediately, it was Gloomsville again but having a male dog as a permanent member of the pack would not have worked out. Even at just ten weeks of age, Buster, who is now called Harvey, was showing the basic instincts.

The Chap and the Boss did their best to fill the sudden gap in my life by keeping me fully occupied with walks, drives and games. Nevertheless, I missed not having any baby to boss about and fuss over, but I had to be philosophical and console myself that that is the way of things. My Magnificent Seven remain my stakes in the future, wherever they may be and, maybe, they will build on my literary breakthrough by becoming authors. My American poet, Bill Bourland, expressed my feelings in a few telling lines:

No chocolate puppy dogs! Will Dido die of grief?
Do not be a silly ass – gosh what a relief!
I well may go and visit them – from time to time, let's say
But after introductory sniffs I'll want to get away.
So don't shed any tears for me – I'm better off without 'em
I'll simply plug my desk-top in and write a book about 'em.

In fact, I quickly recovered my figure and felt feminine again, but in my own mind I will never be the same. I am now a mature bitch – a bitch of the world – and have received my first fan letters addressed to Madame

Dido. Still, there is nothing to stop me behaving like a pup when the mood takes me. It's not impossible that, one day, I might even induce the Chap to let me have another litter. I may be a trifle mature by then but, 'Oh that Bugler!' Meanwhile, I'll drown my sorrows in work and press on with being a career girl.

5 Royal Connections

The Queen can do no wrong (in my eyes)

Both the Chap and I felt that the Queen, as a lover of Labradors, might like to read *One Dog and Her Man*. The Royal Corgis may be the courtier dogs, living at court and seizing the headlines when the two bands of them – known to the Royals as 'Mods and Rockers' – gang up and fight. Indeed, the Queen was bitten, with some loss of blood royal, and needed three stitches in her left hand while attempting to stop a Corgi squabble. It was that incident which made me glad that the paperback rights of my book had been sold to Bantam Books and not to Corgi! No wonder that Her Majesty loves her Labradors. There is little she enjoys more than working them at pheasant shoots and I'd wager that she has never been bitten by one of them. They are never in the royal doghouse, at least not on that score. I don't suppose that Her Majesty feeds her Labradors as, I am told, she feeds her Corgis herself, mixing the food individually. I wonder if they know the difference between a tiara and a headscarf. When she comes in with a headscarf they should know that they are in with a chance of a walk. With a tiara? Not a hope!

The Queen also takes great pleasure in watching gun-dog trials, especially when her own Labradors are competing. However, the Chap understood that it was just not permissible to send her a book directly or, if one did send a copy, it might end up in a pile of unread volumes, as she may receive so many. So, cunning as he is, he awaited an opportunity which duly presented itself during a visit we paid to Sandringham to watch a gun-dog trial run by the *Shooting Times*, a magazine for which the Chap writes occasionally. The Queen's head-keeper there, a friendly Scotsman called Bill Meldrum, is also a famous Labrador trainer and handler and, though I did not compete in the trial, he took a fancy to me, patting my head when I made friends with Topper, a black Labrador belonging to the Queen, which was showing off his skill. Unfortunately, Topper, who rarely makes a mistake in the real shooting field, was misled by a dummy rabbit, deliberately thrown in his path when he was sent to retrieve a dummy pheasant. I was able to sympathize with him, in a dog-to-dog talk, especially when Mr Meldrum's wife, Annie, ran an older dog called Bray, which was not fooled to the slightest degree by the rabbit and did a perfect retrieve. Nobody, dog or man, likes losing face.

Naturally, the Chap mentioned my book to Mr Meldrum and then sent him a copy signed by us both to a rather impressive address – The Queen's Kennels, Sandringham! He liked it so much that he thought Her Majesty might too. So, through his good offices, a copy was eventually put right into the Queen's hand.

We had signed it, 'With loyal respects from Chapman Pincher and loyal love from Dido', and sealed it with my pawprint. Imagine my surprise and delight when the Chap received a letter from Buckingham Palace which read:

The Queen has now received a copy of *One Dog and Her Man* which you and Dido kindly sent her, and which she looks forward to enjoying. Her Majesty well remembers meeting you, though she cannot recall having made Dido's acquaintance. She sends her warm thanks to you both for your kind thought and for inscribing the book to her.

You have to paw it to the Chap! As he says, 'Who dares wins!' Or, as I put it, 'You have to risk it to get the biscuit!' He then went on to explain how, on the one occasion at Windsor when I might well have been presented, I had to be left in the car because I had come into season at the wrong moment. As it was a hot day the windows had to be left open and I fear that my scent, wafting across the trials ground, may have affected the performance of some of the competitors. After all, who would want to concentrate on a dummy when something alive and much more interesting was on hand?

Her Majesty had not been present during our Sandringham visit, for which I had been given an anti-heat injection to make sure that I would not blot my copybook again. So I just lived in hope that another occasion might arise when I might be presented like a dog deb. It nearly happened when we attended the *Shooting Times* Gun-Dog Weekend in Windsor Great Park on 26 April 1992. We arrived a little late and saw a group of half a dozen people watching the Windsor Park keepers showing how not to shoot – with blank cartridges – as a lesson in safety and good manners. We spotted the Duke of Wellington, whose great ancestor is known to all schoolboys for his rubber boots, if for nothing else, and, as we had met him a few times, we tagged ourselves on to the group to watch the fun. Minutes later, when someone began to take photographs, we realized that we were in the royal party with the Queen in front, six feet away! She didn't see us because she was in stitches at the antics of the idiot who kept shooting, dangerously, at low birds – simulated by dummies. I hoped she might notice me and say, 'Is that Dido?' when she said farewell but she didn't, even though my name is printed in large letters on my collar. Anyway, the Duke gave me a nice pat and after we sent him a copy of my book he sent a very friendly letter.

I also met Mr Meldrum again there and he was very kind about my book. Then I was allowed to sit at the table for lunch which I did very quietly, being rewarded by one of the waitresses who slipped me a few titbits. All in all I had a lovely day. I trust the Queen did too. We shall be sending her a copy of this book by the same channel. As the Boss hails from close to Sandringham we may be going there again soon so I may deliver it by paw.

Meanwhile, I wonder if I am the first dog to have had a book read by the Queen. Her Majesty is certainly not the only royal to read it. Her Majesty the Queen Mother, who passed on her love of dogs to her daughter, graciously accepted a copy of my paperback with me on the front cover after one of her closest friends suggested that we should send her one. We received a very nice letter from Scotland, where she was staying, saying that the book was 'delightful'.

The Duke of Fife, who is in the line of succession, though now distant, bought seven copies of *One Dog and Her Man* to give to friends. I had met him before when he came to dinner at our house and we met again in August 1991 at Kinnaird, a luxury hotel near Dunkeld in Scotland, where we were all attending an open-air concert. The Duke brought a photograph of his chocolate Labrador, Louis, who looked so like me that, on seeing me again, he immediately ordered one of my pups.

I thought that I might be meeting Princess Anne when we arrived to shoot in Lincolnshire and found that another expected guest was her husband, Mark Philips. However, she was not with him and, as there was an estrangement, he did not talk about her much, though he was very nice to me. As happened with me, his dogs had to sleep in the car that night so we had a few friendly barks at each other. It's funny whom you meet out shooting!

I have also met another non-royal husband of a princess – that very nice Sir Angus Ogilvy who is married to Princess Alexandra. We have met at several shoots and he has always been very kind. The last time, when were all at Broadlands, our loader was the former head-keeper to Sir Thomas Sopwith, a friend of the Chap's before my time. (I'm sorry I missed Sir Thomas and his wife because at their country house visiting dogs were not only allowed in but could sleep on the bed!) The keeper amused us all by reminding Sir Angus how Princess Alexandra had served as a beater at Sir Thomas's shoot and how he had insisted on paying her with the other beaters at the end of the day. When she took the money – I think it was about £3 in those days – she bemoaned the fact that she had never been paid before for all the other times she had done her best to put birds over guns. I sent Sir Angus and his delightful princess a copy of my paperback and we got a warm reply from him, hand-written from St James's Palace.

When picking up the Chap's granddaughter, Helen, from her boarding-school at Cold Ash, I also briefly met Prince and Princess Michael of Kent who were looking at the school as a possible place for their own daughter. The Chap used to shoot with the Prince but it was before my time, otherwise I would have known him better because, no doubt, I would have chased after his pheasants. The Boss remembers him best for a remark he made when, after a very cold pheasant drive at Ramsbury Manor, he found her trying to thaw out, sitting with her Wellington boots close to a brazier kindly set up by one of the keepers. 'Ah sole bonne femme!' he observed. My kind of wit, I fear.

Anyway, we sent the Prince a copy of my paperback and he sent a very nice reply from Kensington Palace, beginning 'My dear friend', which I am sure meant me, and remarking that I certainly have a 'signature of distinction'.

The Boss received a nice letter about me from the Countess of Harewood whose husband, the Earl, has royal blood, his mother having been the former Princess Royal. She said that she had owned a chocolate Labrador called Cleo (short for Cleopatra) because all the Harewood pet dogs were named after characters in opera, on which the Earl is very keen. For this reason she had even owned a dog called Dido, after the opera by Purcell, but she was only a Poodle.

The Chap, stupidly, messed up a chance for me to meet Princess Margaret. It arose suddenly on a Sunday morning but the Chap felt too weary to drag himself out to lunch. Opportunity had knocked but all the Chap did was to complain of the noise!

There is only one thing that makes me a little concerned about the Chap's loyalty to the House of Windsor. Whenever he puts a stamp on a letter he bangs on the Queen's head so hard that a psychologist might have some funny interpretation, suspecting, perhaps, that he is really a Republican deep down, though I doubt that. It always brings me running, as though it was a case of dog save the Queen, but the truth is that after the fifth or sixth banging I know I will shortly be going out when he takes his letters to the post.

I have met some of the old European royalty in the shooting field, such as various Hapsburg Archdukes, including Archduke Rudolf – grand-nephew of the Emperor Franz Josef, who ruled over a huge area of Europe. They are very nice but smell the same as ordinary people to me. It's the same with my friend Count Tolstoy, who hails from the Russian aristocracy.

I was also with the Chap when he visited the Duke of Marlborough in his private lair at Blenheim Palace. As we arrived a little early and I was very pregnant, he asked one of the servants for permission to run me in the park, though there was a notice proclaiming that all dogs must be kept on leads. 'If the Duke knows you that will be OK!' he said. So, once again, I was treated as a VID, while the ordinary visitors gave us funny looks as they walked their dogs on leads. Later, the Duke was charmed to receive a copy of *One Dog and Her Man* signed by both of us.

Sorry if I appear to name-drop but I do enjoy it.

6 My White House Friend

Let us now praise famous dogs

Not many dogs have received a communication from the most powerful man in the world but I have. It arrived in the form of a card from the White House signed by President George Bush and also by his nice wife, Barbara. 'You were kind to remember us in such a special way,' it stated. 'We sincerely appreciate your thoughtfulness and we send you our best wishes.'

It came in response to a copy of *One Dog and Her Man* which I had sent to the Bush's Springer Spaniel, Millie, because she, too, had published a book about the ups and downs of life as the First Bitch, ghosted by her mistress. The card was accompanied by a lovely colour photograph of Millie sitting, with a ball in her mouth, right in the middle of the White House tulips — something I would not be allowed to do. Nor would I be permitted to hunt squirrels in the garden as she was. Actually, it is a delight we share because the grey squirrels I see out walking are the same species as those in the garden in Washington, having been introduced here. I am permitted then, even encouraged, to chase them because the Chap says they are pests, damaging trees and stealing birds' eggs. Yet he regards a grey squirrel in the garden as a fascinating visitor and, somehow, I am supposed to appreciate the difference. It is the same with a red squirrel when we see one in Scotland. He calls me off yet, to me, being colour blind, all squirrels are grey. Millie complained that there are no squirrels at the Bush's holiday home in Kennebunkport, in Maine. That must be just about the only place they have not penetrated.

Later, when I heard that Millie was poorly with some auto-immune disease, I sent her a 'Get well' card. Apart from the fact that Millie is a sister author, I felt that I should do all I could to foster Anglo-American accord, especially as my ancestors hailed from the same continent. I also feel some special kinship with her because she is partly a chocolate dog, though in her breed the fanciers call the colour liver and white instead of chocolate and white. I must say that I think chocolate is nicer. Liver is lovely to eat but not to look like. And is it cooked liver or raw?

It was odd that Millie should have fallen ill because both President Bush and his wife happened to be suffering from thyrotoxicosis which is also regarded as an auto-immune disease. The coincidence was being looked at by physicians and medical researchers last time I checked, though I don't think that anyone infected anybody else. Anyway, all three seem to be all right now. I do hope that I don't catch anything from the Chap.

Millie's book, called *Millie's Story*, about life at the top in the White House, was different from mine in many ways, being more of a picture book. It also sold far more, not only making the author the most famous dog in America, including film-star dogs, but earned 890,000 dollars in 1991 – more than half of the Bush's gross income that year. (When addressing some students the President said, 'Study hard and you might become President but, even then, you'll never make as much money as your dog.') Of course, Millie had a head and four paws start over me by virtue of her social and professional position. She met everyone of importance who visited the White House. They made a ritual fuss whether they liked dogs or not though, like me, she can surely detect those who are just putting on an act. She attended top-secret morning briefings in the Oval Office with the man she called 'the Prez', though she must have another name for him after his defeat in the election. (I wonder if the KGB ever thought of fitting her with a bug to make her into the 'Third Dog'? Or if the security men checked her out just in case they had? And whether she was swept electronically, from time to time, as a matter of routine?) There is also built-in media interest in White House dogs going back to the day when a former President, Lyndon Johnson, earned world-wide obloquy by being photographed picking up his dog by the ears! When Millie had puppies, for instance, she appeared on the front cover of *Life* magazine. Nevertheless, another magazine selected her as Washington's ugliest dog showing, as even the Chap agrees, these days, the Press is not to be trusted.

Mrs Bush donated all Millie's royalties to her special charity, called the Literacy Foundation, to help people to learn to read and write. Guess where most of my royalties went – to the Chap, who believes that charity begins at home though I got my share of it in different ways.

We were surprised that the President did not make much use of Millie's popularity during his campaign to get re-elected, apart from claiming that she knew more about foreign affairs than his opponents. The

Chap would have exploited mine. Naturally, we were rooting for Bush and my White House mole and when he was defeated I wrote to Millie sympathizing with her loss of status and hoping that there would be squirrels in her new home. Her predicament was not lost on the American cartoonists. One of them labelled a drawing of George Bush explaining the consequences of his defeat to Millie as 'The Really Hard Part'. I suppose her summary eviction from the White House should be a lesson to me to keep out of politics. Although the ex-President is a keen fisherman, like the Chap, and will be doing more now, I don't think that Millie goes with him, so I am one up there.

No doubt, the publishers are pressing her to do another book but I do not think that she is going to be prolific, as I intend to be. I suspect that she lacks the discipline. And now that she is no longer the First Bitch her sales are likely to suffer without that cachet. Maybe Millie's departure from the American literary scene will make room for me there. It's an ill wind that blows no dog some good and one has to be realistic about one's career in this highly competitive world.

What has fame done for Millie? Like me, she remains the same dog at heart but I agree with her that, now we have made the headlines, it is no longer a question of whom we know but who knows us.

7 A Dog of Means

Put not your trust in money but put your money in trust

Once my contract with my publisher had been signed the first tranche of my royalties (I wonder why they call them that) became payable, so the Chap thought it only fair that I should have my own bank account into which the money could be paid, so that I might become a dog of independent means. But was there any precedent for this? Would a bank account in a dog's name be legally possible? The Chap decided to find out by writing, formally, to the manager of Lloyds Bank in Hungerford, where he has his own account.

The manager took the request most seriously, consulting various authoritative books on the laws of contract. He decided that, in the eyes of the law, I did not possess 'contractual capacity' but provided I had trust in the Chap and he had trust in me, which we both had, then we could open a joint account styled 'Chapman Pincher–Dido Joint Venture Account'.

The bank manager stressed that the mutual trust had to be genuine otherwise, if I suspected that the Chap might abscond with the money, it would be necessary for trustees to be appointed. When we went to see him he was left in no doubt of our mutual trust so it was agreed that a joint account would be in legal order and, with the butcher just a few yards up the road from our house, the idea of a joint account had instant appeal for me. We finally settled for a Joint Deposit Account with twelve days' notice which meant that we would get extra money called interest. I like to think of it earning interest while I just enjoy myself. As long as I stay in the black I'll stay in the bones – and the chocolate drops.

Before we arrived at the bank, at noon on the appointed day, to open the account, an interviewer and camera crew from Coast-to-Coast Television, which covered much of the South of England, had been to our house to take shots of us both at work on the word processor and walking in the churchyard and on the canal tow-path. Then, when we all moved to the bank in Hungerford High Street – the site of the sad massacre – the local Press was already in attendance, sensing a good photo-opportunity, and so was a representative from *Lloyds Bank News*, which goes to all Lloyds' branches and is widely read by the staff. There was also a little crowd outside, wondering what was going on.

I was not averse to some constructive publicity, especially as dogdom was suffering such a bad press at the time through all the row about savage breeds, which was really just because a few wrong dogs had been in the wrong place at the wrong time. We had taken my paw-stamp to enable me to sign my pawtograph and I was photographed doing it in the office of the manager, Robin Wilde. When the formalities had been completed and both the Chap and I had signed the documents, Mr Wilde confirmed, on TV, that no other dog had ever opened an account there though, from time to time, some dogs had left deposits!

I was then photographed banking my first royalty cheque and then withdrawing £2 from the account to celebrate by treating myself to a steak and was disappointed to find what a small amount it bought. However, it was reassuring to know that I was now a dog of independent means and not just a kept bitch. It was not possible to provide me with a plastic card to use the cash machine if I happened to be passing but, if necessary, I could go to the bank on my own as the cashiers there all know me. However, I prefer to use one of my messengers – usually the Boss.

As I have said, the *Newbury Weekly News* published a story next day headlined, 'Dido's barking all the way to the bank!' (they didn't think of 'Rich Bitch') accompanied by a picture showing me at the counter with my paw-print being used to make my first withdrawal from the cashier, Miss Hayley Beard, who has since become a friend. 'The clever canine had clearly collared the idea of making the best of her money, having decided to put it into a deposit account,' the report stated.

Within a few days, as the Chap had predicted, we received begging letters from various charities but they were all ignored because he knew my view – cast your bread upon the water and the ducks will eat it.

Lloyds Bank News did me proud with a lovely colour picture of me shaking hands with the manager on being welcomed on the doorstep of the bank. Even the Lloyds Bank Chief Executive, Brian Pitman, who is a friend of the Chap, wrote to say that he was proud to have me as a customer and looked forward to 'a long and happy relationship with Dido'. He thought my book was a 'super idea'. Perhaps, one day, if my fame continues, I may supplant that black horse in the Lloyds logo. That would be a triumph!

When nothing appeared on our TV set for almost a week the Chap and the Boss feared that my great event was not going to be screened after all and, knowing how disappointed the Lloyds staff were likely to be after all the fuss, they daren't go into the bank. Fortunately, when they switched on one evening there was jubilation, for it was announced that I would be appearing later in the programme. In fact, *Coast-to-Coast* did me really proud, devoting several minutes of top viewing time showing me at work with the Chap in his study, out researching my next book and opening the account at the bank.

Like most authors I have been astonished to learn how little we earn for such long labour. As the Chap puts it, 'There has to be an easier way of not making a living.' However, now that translation rights have been sold to Germany and Japan, hopefully with more to come, I can dream of becoming affluent. I'd certainly take no offence at being called a rich bitch.

Meanwhile, I have had to be reasonably understanding when the Chap has occasionally raided the joint account to withdraw his share of the royalties. A dog and her money are soon parted! I thought I had it well in paw but the labourer is worthy of his hire, and I suppose I should do my share to keep the old boy in the style to which he is accustomed. I concede that my royalties are for the general benefit of the pack – so long as the Chap realizes that, by the same token, so are his. I have also learned the wisdom underlying the Chap's mournful moan, 'Whatever you may earn there will always be someone waiting for it.'

The Chap was becoming concerned about the possibility that I might have a serious problem on my paws through being taxed on my meagre royalties and even more worried that he might be taxed on them. So he decided to seek advice from the Treasury. His letter asking whether a dog which has produced a book and is in receipt of royalties can be registered as a tax payer was passed to Inland Revenue headquarters at Somerset House. Eventually, the Press Officer, Tim Morris, replied that the Revenue's presumption would be that the income belonged to the owner of the dog (which I think is unfair) and that he would have to pay the tax (which is OK by me). If the Chap claimed that I should pay the tax he would have to prove that I had entered into a royalty agreement. He would also have to prove that I had physically written the book, which I think is also unfair because lots of famous people have books written for them by ghost writers for a set fee and then take the royalties and any other proceeds.

The Inland Revenue also pointed out that if we got bogged down in argument about who had really written the book, it might be concluded that neither of us had and the money would be snatched by the Crown as profits belonging to no person. 'That should give you paws for thought,' Mr Morris added. It did.

I don't think that the Queen would approve of my money being snatched, even by the Crown but, on the other hand, I do not think that it would be constitutional for her to interfere, much as she loves her canine subjects. Having listened to the Chap's views on rapacious lawyers, which he expresses in such lurid language, I am sure that we should avoid any legal action with the taxman or with anyone else for that matter. I have heard of one heartening case though it was a long time ago. It concerns a dog belonging the Eighth Earl of Home which was a dab paw at catching salmon, having once landed twenty, unaided, in a morning. The fishing on the opposite bank was owned by Lord Tankerville, an irascible old man, who regarded the dog as a poacher and prosecuted it, the case being listed as 'Lord Tankerville v a dog, the property of the Earl of Home'. To its everlasting glory the dog won!

In spite of that precedent, it looks like the Chap will have to cough up, to which he is well used, claiming that death, taxes and injustice are the only certainties in life. I have no doubt that he will pay it out of my earnings which, I suppose, is fair enough. As to what should be left for me, since my paws are too big to operate an electronic calculator, I'll have to work it out by dogarithms.

The Chap replied to Mr Morris pointing out that I proposed to refer to the tax position in my next book as there was no harm in letting the public see that the Inland Revenue has a sense of humour. He asked whether a dog had ever been registered for tax before as a tax evasion stunt but got a dusty answer showing that either the Inland Revenue's patience or its sense of humour had been exhausted. You would think that a lifetime of raking in other people's money would make them ever joyful. Anyway, they can't take away our greatest reward – all the new friends the book has made us.

If I earned a great deal of money I could not become a tax exile because I couldn't get back into the country without six months' quarantine, which is a most unfair discrimination because many humans bring in dangerous diseases like malaria and AIDS without being quarantined. I don't think the Chap would emigrate with me because he is too much of an Anglophile but there are people who go to great lengths on behalf of their dogs. Until recently there was a nice young man in Kintbury who had a beautiful Rhodesian Ridgeback, with whom I became friendly on our walks. One day he told us that he was emigrating 'for as long as my dog remains alive'. When asked what he meant he said, 'I could never come back to Britain and leave him abroad with somebody else but when he is no more I will probably return.' What a splendid sentiment!

I am just waiting for the day when somebody who doesn't really know the Chap and thinks that anything is for sale at the right price offers to buy me. The Chap might keep his temper or, as is more likely, I might learn some new words.

He may be sarcastic on many issues but he does not fit Oscar Wilde's definition of a cynic as someone who knows the price of everything but the value of nothing. On the contrary, he says that both my price and my value are infinite.

The Chap says that there is a much-dreaded Jewish curse which bad fairies pronounce at the birth of a child – 'May you be the only rich member of a poor family!' Fortunately, mine all seem reasonably well fixed.

8 The Canine Predicament

Dog is the measure of all things

Being a dog in a man's – and a woman's – world poses problems. Being Dido poses particular problems, especially for the Chap. He says that if he's a bumpkin, an awkward country fellow, as he unquestionably is, then I'm a dumpkin – an awkward country dog. Well, letting that pass, I'm certainly not 'just a dog', a human concept I heartily deplore. For a start, I am a unique individual and a Labrador! In 1991 the Labrador was easily the most popular breed registered at the Kennel Club, having, so rightly, overtaken the Yorkshire Terrier. And this was in the depths of a recession when small dogs are much cheaper to feed. We have been steady favourites for years and now people have finally got their priorities completely right. I will do what I can to keep us in the Number One position – I owe it to the human race as well as to my own – but like all previous Top Dogs, such as the Cocker Spaniel and the miniature Poodle, we could be deposed by the human whim you call 'fashion' because you follow each other like sheep.

To us fashion seems an extraordinary human folly. For the sake of a peaceful life we have to be obedient up to a point, but the great mass of you slavishly obey what you are told to do by authority or what custom and fashion decree. A few people, whose object is to make money, compel millions to do their bidding by inducing them to change their taste in clothes, for instance. We would never willingly be manipulated like that. Fashion has been thrust on some of my race like the poor Poodle, which is shorn to look like a topiary tree, with horrible and totally unnatural bare patches and I cannot believe that it likes it. It is an offence to its dignity and dignity is something we care about, especially we Labradors.

While I have the further distinction of being a chocolate Labrador, a colour so unusual that many people stop to ask about it, fashion has been against it. Though my colour is as old as the breed – some of the first Labradors imported into Britain were chocolate – some dog judges are biased against it, though not against chocolate Spaniels. This colour prejudice was made clear to us by several competitors at Cruft's when we took part in the show in 1992. 'What is so special about black and yellow?' they asked. Happily, though, the best Labrador pup in the show that year proved to be a chocolate. So you see why I feel that I am not only working for dogdom but for chocolate dogdom, in particular.

In addition to being a chocolate Labrador I am, above all, *me* – a unique creation like all of you. Just as the sort-out of your genes at conception ensures that no two human beings, not even twins, are ever exactly alike, neither are two dogs. At this point, for new readers, I should say a little about me. I recently celebrated my fifth birthday with a cake with five candles on it, though, as I was in the process of being slimmed down after my phantom pregnancy, you can guess who ate almost all of it. I am properly dog-shaped as nature intended, for the Labrador breed has not been seriously interfered with by breeders and is free from the many follies of the dog 'fancy'. Nevertheless, a few bad genes, which would have been quickly weeded out by the survival of only the fittest in the wild, have crept in through the domestic breeding process. These have given rise to hip and eye problems but, happily, not in my case or those of my forbears.

By nature I am a happy dog, not given to looking cowed or miserable. On the contrary I am a smiler, much more so than the Chap, in fact. He has the kind of face that when he's fed up it shows. Mine doesn't, though I have to admit that I have my moods and sometimes, though never for long, I haven't a word to throw to a man. Nor am I ever ill-tempered or barkless with rage like the Chap, though the Boss says he has mellowed in recent years, no doubt due to my benign influence. I am also kind by nature, to both humans and my own species, being all for the underdog and even more so for the underbitch. I admit that I am exuberant but that's no bad thing when there is too little exuberance in the world. I reckon that we could do with more of it.

'Am I humanized?' you may ask. I suppose that because of my very close relationship with the Chap I am humanized more than most dogs and have to confess that, not being aggressive, I don't think that I would last long in the wild. On the other hand, my especially close observation of human character might make me more cunning and more ruthless. Without question, you lot have made an enormous impact on us and on our culture but we have done the same with yours. As I will explain, I have good reasons for not wishing to be too human. We are both adapted to our different needs and I suspect that we are better adapted than you, perhaps, because we have been on earth longer.

My behaviour repeatedly shows that my intelligence is well above average, to say the least. For example, the two flap doors, through which I can find my way into the garden, can each be locked with a key which used to be turned and left in the lock when others intended that I should be kept in. Not any more! I learned how to turn the key so now they have to remove it. As further evidence, when we went to visit a house where there is a swing-door between the dining room and the kitchen I found my way through to the smell of the food in five minutes. A Labrador which had lived there for several years had never once had the wit to push hard enough against the door to open it.

When we are walking on the river, or elsewhere, and I come to a fork in the path – being usually a few yards ahead – I always wait there to see which the Chap will choose. Further, I position myself on the side of the fork which I would prefer. This usually works in my favour, either because the Chap wants to oblige me or because, seeing me in position, he subconsciously accepts my choice. I am good at both geography and at getting my own way.

A good memory is another aspect of being intelligent and I have proved that I have that on many occasions which I will describe as this book unfolds. As one example, I suppose that I pick up no more than about three ticks a year, but no sooner does the Chap get out the can of spare petrol to make a tick release its hold than I am off, remembering, full well, the sting the drops of petrol cause. I even get suspicious when I see him get the little brush he uses to anoint the tick. I am told that some magazine devised an IQ test for dogs but I see no reason whatever to submit to one, any more than the Chap does to prove that he is not stupid.

What seems to be stupid behaviour to you usually has a sensible canine explanation, like barking at sounds which, with your inferior acoustic equipment, you cannot hear, or making funny noises when, in fact, what I am doing is thinking aloud. As for barking in general, I always bark my mind but I do my best to comply with the Chap's edict when he wags his finger at me with 'One wuff is enuff!' even though I may profoundly disagree, especially when he makes so much noise himself. After all, I am only 'communicating', which psychologists regard as so important. The freedom to bark is one of the great democratic freedoms of dog. Dogs have died for it. And, as I always think, if you can't bark in Berkshire where can you bark?

Some of the human stupidities we witness are much grosser than anything we perpetrate. One of the biggest, happily not committed by my lot but often seen in the shooting field, is the belief that beating will make us more obedient. It certainly isn't done to strike a lady, though some dog owners do so. Spare the dog and rod the child if you must take your frustration out on somebody because, at least, he might understand why he is getting it.

There is a movement to make the slapping of a naughty child illegal yet, at the same time, children are being starved, shot and blown up all over the world. Compared with man's inhumanity to man, and with some men's inanimality to animals, dog's incaninity to dog is as nothing. If we were in the habit of shaking our heads in bewilderment, as you humans are, we would never stop. The main activity of the primitive ancestors of both of us was killing for food and we both remain saddled with that aggressive trait, but now that it no longer serves a purpose, we have almost eliminated it. You have not. In fact, the history of your so-called civilization is a shameful record of the killing and destruction of your own species, which still goes on, with ever-increasing refinement of the methods for doing it. Torture is a uniquely human invention. Dogs would never indulge in it though cats get near it when they play with a mouse.

There are more breeds of dog than there are human races but we have never hated or attacked each other on such a scale. No dog born of bitch would dream of doing such a thing. Within dogdom there is no indiscriminate destruction, no exploitation, no racialism, no prejudice, no snobbism. We are truly an international species. With us, a dog's a dog for a' that, wherever he might live or come from. On reflection, it could be argued that dog shows, in which breeds are separated and eventually compete for the Supreme Championship, are racist, but that is not our doing. Certainly, if anything comparable was done on a human racial basis in the Miss World or Mister Universe competitions, the outcry from certain quarters would be deafening.

Sadly, your exploitation and killing are not confined to your own species. Never in our history did we hunt another species to extinction, because it would have been madness to do so, but *Homo sapiens* has extinguished thousands, from the mammoth onwards to the elephant, rhino, whale and dolphin, which are seriously threatened. The time is ripe for a new Charles Darwin to write *The Termination of Species*. Or perhaps I should do it.

We never delude each other or ourselves as you do, so much of your time. I have heard a grossly overweight man say, 'That dog's too fat. You are giving it too much to eat.' Another man, with a florid face which had cost a fortune, observed of a nice Dalmatian friend of mine, in censorious tone, 'That dog's no good for breeding. It's got a pink nose.' Then there was the ludicrous situation on the bank of a salmon river when the Chap became irritated because I was a bit slow in answering his call. There he was, standing in his great clod-hopping waders, and guess what he said to me – 'You are getting too big for your boots!'

He uses a lot of expressions which don't seem very intelligent to me. For instance, he often says I am full of beans. But nobody in his right mind would feed beans to a dog that lives in the house, if you get my meaning. He is also prone to say that I'm on the pig's back, but that would be a funny sight even if I could stay on. Then he might say, after publishing some controversial statement, 'I hope I don't have to eat my words.' How can you eat words? Come to think, though, I suppose that we who earn our bread by the pen (the word processor these days), do eat our words.

Though the Chap prides himself on his 'scientific' approach to life I hear him making the wildest assumptions. When he comes down in the morning and I am still curled up on the beanbag he will tell the Boss, 'The lazy old so-and-so hasn't moved all night.' Then, hours later, he finds the big hole in the garden which I dug while they were asleep. The question he should ask himself is, 'Why is she so tired?' Then the answer might dawn on him.

I reckon that I make particularly intelligent use of my senses. Take my stare, for instance. Most dogs fail to realize the full potential of the canine stare. Human beings cannot stand much of it and, eventually, unless they are totally insensitive, will do what a dog wants to get rid of it. Just by staring long enough I can make the Chap feel guilty, greedy, lazy, penitent, generous or affectionate. He really is a sucker for a stare. Like a woman's tears, it is a powerful weapon in a bitch's armoury and can be refined with experience.

In fact, various aspects of canine sight never cease to fascinate the Chap. Take, for instance, my ability to recognize other dogs, whatever their size or shape, though I may never have seen the breed before, and even from a long distance and from inside a closed car. Humans could easily see that pygmies were of the same species, but would tiny people be seen as human beings if they were as small and peculiarly shaped as, say, a miniature Dachshund? I doubt it.

For a few months, one of our neighbours had an orphan lamb, called Dandy, which walked around the village on a lead and appeared to think that it was a dog. When taken down to a field full of sheep it had no interest in them but clearly identified with the dog which lived in the same house. I don't know what that dog thought but I did not mistake Dandy for a dog for one moment. When we were asked to the show-jumping ground at Hickstead by the owner, Douglas Bunn, which sounded a promising name, I was introduced to some mini-horses which were no bigger than dogs but they did not fool me, even from a distance, any more than I fooled them. We simply took no interest in each other at all. (The day was memorable for another reason, though. One of the jumping horses was called Fido Dido though, sadly, it didn't win.)

Oddly, perhaps, dogs on TV mean nothing to me – not even when I see myself on the box as I did after Cruft's. (That could, of course, be modesty. I'm not saying, one way or the other.) However, I received a letter from a Yorkie, called Suzy, who watches the screen on the look-out for dogs so that she can give them a bark or a growl. Her owner claims that she can even recognize cartoon dogs, including that ridiculous looking creature who, sitting in a chair, advertises Ceefax. I suppose there must be something in it because somebody has marketed a video specially made for dogs with dogs in it. But, for me, a flat image on a screen with no smell still means nothing.

In spite of my accomplishments you may still say that I am only a dog but I've got things going for me and two of them are the Chap and the Boss, the other members of my pack. Dogs have contrived to mould human beings to their purpose far more than any other species. Apart from being my waiters, my valets, my walkers and my minders, the Boss and the Chap are also my chauffeurs. Which human star or which rich woman has two chauffeurs? They even hold the door open to enable me to get in and out and close it after me, as good chauffeurs should but which the Chap often forgets to do for the Boss. Further, with the Chap who is teetotal, I have a chauffeur who could never fail a breath test.

It is, of course, a give-and-take situation and I do my share for the common cause. I am the Chap's right-hand dog, for instance, and as the Boss is a southpaw, I suppose I am her left-hand dog. If ever I sense that they are feeling low or are in need of reassurance, all I have to do is nuzzle them. I fall into the category of a 'pet', being 'a creature kept in the house as a favourite', but, since the Chap and the Boss are also animals – they are not plants and you have to be one or the other – I am justified in regarding them as my pets, to be fondled and made a fuss of when it suits me and to be ignored when it does not.

In fact, of course, the relationship is a mutual commitment and unique in the living world, which makes me feel very superior to other animals in just being a dog, and an only dog at that, there being no other in this household once my pups departed to their various homes.

I'm not going to be exploited but I am wise enough to know that I live, literally, in a command economy – 'Do this', 'Don't do that' – and must obey the pack rules (up to a point) whenever I hear Chapman speak out loud and bold. So I can never be entirely pawloose and fancy free but, by not pushing my luck and using the wiles which nature has given me, I contrive to get my way on the things that matter. The secret, of course, lies in the skill of inducing the Chap to delude himself into believing that we are doing what *he* wants. The Boss is equally skilful at this and, maybe, it is partly because we are female that we are both so successful.

There is nothing in canine behaviour to compare with human gullibility in general. It is one of man's most consistent features. You can fool a dog for a few minutes but then the trick does not work any more. Yet people go through life buying gold bricks, falling for one expensive food fad, health nostrum or gimmick promise after another. Millions of you believe things called horoscopes, based on the movements of the stars, studiously looking them up each day in newspapers. Surely, if the stars can influence human behaviour they should affect that of every other creature. That inference has recently been taken up by a dog magazine (*Dogs Today*) which prints canine horoscopes so that pets can be told what fate has in store for them. The predictions are based on the Zodiac, the belt of the sky which the sun happens to traverse in the course of the year. Zodiac simply means 'animal circle' and the twelve constellations through which the sun appears to pass – the so-called 'signs' – are mostly based on different creatures which primitive astronomers thought they represented. The Chap is a Ram, which may well be justified. I am a Taurus but the only bull of which I would take notice would have to possess horns. Anyway, I would rather not know what the future holds, surprise being one of the spices of a dog's life.

It is your collective gullibility that, to us, is so incredible and so dangerous. Whole nations, conditioned by mob hysteria, buy gold bricks from politicians under names like Fascism and Communism, suffering terribly as a consequence. They become more enslaved than we have ever been and they have enslaved themselves, while we, perhaps, had no option. Time and again, throughout your history, we dogs have witnessed the incredible situation in which one power-mad man is able to hold millions of you in terrible subjection for many years. That would never happen even in the quite small societies of wild dogs, wolves or other animals. Such a tyrant would be repeatedly challenged and eventually defeated and banished from society while many of yours die in their beds of old age, still in command.

Persistently, you trust the running of your lives to politicians who so often demonstrate their inability to run their own, often laying their whole careers and private lives on the line for a little illicit pleasure. Of course, politicians are not alone in sacrificing their marriages for paltry purposes. Millions do it, with horrible consequences for their dogs who suffer and may be discarded in the breakdown.

In fact, the more I see of the human race in general the more I am left wondering if the title *Homo sapiens* is really deserved. It could only have been bestowed by a man and is a further expression of human vanity. An objectively observant dog would surely have chosen something different for a species characterized by such expressions of unwisdom as gullibility, inhumanity and greed. I would plump for *Homo rapax* – rapacious or greedy man. However, I don't want to be too hard. Man has many admirable and even noble features. And you know what we dogs say – 'Give a man a bad name and hang him.'

9 Lust for Living

A live dog is better than a dead lion
(Or a live one for that matter)

The two aspects of my health about which the Chap and the Boss profess to be consistently concerned are ensuring that I get some exercise and do not get too fat. Labradors are supposed to need to walk eight miles a day to be fully fit. The old Chap does his best and so do I, running around on my own so that I walk at least twice as far as the Chap does, though I suppose that his heart and general condition are in greater need than mine at the moment. The Boss also does her share, taking me shopping and stopping off somewhere to run me in a field if only for a few minutes. Every yard helps, as the old Chap says when he takes me up to the post-box each morning, wet or fine. In fact, I enjoy that little pipe-opener, which takes us back through the village allotments where I can patronize various favourite places, much used by other dogs, while the Chap gossips with the men who do the digging. I suspect that he picks their brains to bone up for a BBC gardening quiz on which he occasionally appears. There are field mice there and sometimes I get a good run at a cat. Early one morning I put up a large roebuck which had been lying down among the vegetables. The end of a stag-night in the cabbages?

I would not leave my bowl of food for any walk but am always prepared to leave a bone on the principle that a walk on the paws is worth two in the expectation. Also, I know that the bone will still be there when I get back. If the Boss has moved it to keep the flies off I always remember and ask for it.

Swimming in the river in the summer also helps to keep me slim and tones me up. I always get my collar wet and sometimes the Chap forgets to take it off. Would a damp collar give me rheumatism? the Boss wonders. The Chap says there is no connection between dampness and rheumatism, that it is another old bitch's tale. I hope he is right but I have had no twinges yet.

Dogs in the wild are rarely obese because they do not have much chance to get fat and would soon run it off anyway. In domesticity (which I prefer to 'captivity', though we are captives) the species *Canis* shows a high incidence of obesity, about one third of the dogs seen by vets in Britain being overweight. Labradors are specially susceptible simply, I suppose, because eating is our favourite activity. I am a particularly good trencherdog, my feeling being that 'one crowded hour of glorious grub would be worth an age without a name' if I could get it. Though humans do spend hours at the table I have never seen any of them wax as excited about food as I do, though I have often seen them get animated about drink. Obviously they don't enjoy it as much as I do or perhaps they are never really as hungry as I am. Just as for any wolf, gluttony is the best policy for any dog because, with life being so full of uncertainties, one cannot be absolutely sure that there will be food tomorrow. The Chap read in the newspaper that an American discovery, called Gotta Bite, which sends fish into a frenzy of feeding, is said to make dogs eat their food more quickly. No need to ask what the Boss commented – 'No Labrador needs that!'

Humans call our gluttony greed but we are only doing what nature equipped us to do. Further, we are not the only ones. I reckon that ducks are even greedier. Those on the canal will go on and on eating bread as long as anyone will throw it to them. There are three old ducks which have learned that the baker puts out bread for birds and, every day, they waddle up past our front door, slowly, to the back of the bakery – the Chap has paced it as 380 yards (more than 3000 duck-steps). Then they gorge themselves and fly back. Surely they've got their priorities wrong! I would fly up to the food and waddle back. Incidentally, we saw five young ducks waddling up from the canal to the baker's the other day. Who told them there was bread there? How did they get the message? Do ducks communicate like bees which, according to the Chap, tell other bees where nectar is by waggling their behinds? This gives some idea of the distance and direction of nectar-bearing flowers which the waggler has discovered. Ducks never stop waggling their behinds. Perhaps I have made a new biological discovery.

While on the subject of greed, your species is in a class on its own. I am not thinking just about food. Greed for money, which is far more reprehensible, is ruining your environment – and ours and that of every other creature – by burning forests, uprooting hedges and polluting the air, rivers and seas to an extent which could eventually kill us all. You are even turning the gentle rain into corrosive acid that destroys the trees on which we all depend for oxygen to breathe. If some enemy from outer space was doing it the peoples of the world would unite to put a stop to it. Instead you go on doing it in the names of 'progress' and 'prosperity'. We would never do anything so lunatic.

I must say that the quality of the food service here, at Church House, merits four stars. Whenever I return from an outing at any time after 4 p.m. my bowl of food is waiting for me, outside or in the conservatory if it is raining, and I am very surprised and disappointed if it is not. Humans say that everything comes to she who waits but patience, like moderation, is a virtue I might, fleetingly, admire in others. I prefer to hasten things by agitating, though not too brashly, because I have found that it is counter-productive to upset my staff. However, there appear to be dogs who are treated with even greater deference. One Labrador I have heard tell about, called Mr Fritz, who lives in my native Devon, sits at the dining-room table with the other guests and with his paws on it, being served like anybody else. Quite right too, though few of us reach that degree of privilege.

While the Chap and the Boss go to great lengths to make sure that everything I eat is fresh, we dogs enjoy flesh which is distinctly on the high side. This harks back to the days when we had to eat carrion if there was no fresh food to be had. Occasionally I indulge myself in this traditional food if I find a stinking dead fish on the river bank or a dead rabbit on the common. The vets call it 'depraved appetite' and the Chap invariably lumbers up crying, 'Leave it! Leave it!' then makes me disgorge anything I am in the process of swallowing. He then bangs on about the stink, yet it does not smell much worse than the grouse he sometimes eats or some of those cheeses by which he sets such store. Perhaps that depraved taste harks back to the days when his primitive ancestors were driven to eat carrion and found that they liked it.

What really infuriates him is if I roll in it, which I have taken to doing recently. Why, I can't explain. All I know is that I get a compulsory bath which I dislike or, in summer, am immediately taken down to the river, though I regard that as a reward.

My regular rations come out of a can and I like them very much. As I shall describe later, I've seen the tinned food made and the care and research that goes into it. Further, in the Chap's determination to 'put himself in my skin' he has tasted what I get, though only after he was assured by the makers that ingredients unfit for human consumption are never used. He pronounced it 'just like cold stew' which, of course, he would prefer hot. I just say that it's a poor stomach that won't warm it.

While it is the Boss who usually feeds me I noticed, recently, that the Chap seemed unusually keen to do it. It transpired that the tins of Pedigree Chum we had acquired were all marked on the top, 'Is there a car in this can?' The inside of the lid of fifty lucky tins announced that the purchaser had won a nice motor car so, though the Chap had never won anything in his life, he was still hopeful. If we had won a car, whose would it have been? Mine, surely. It was all my food bought out of my book royalties after one of the Chap's raids on my bank account. Anyway, we didn't win one. As the Chap says, all three of us will have to go on slogging for everything we get.

I also like tinned tripe which was no hardship for the Chap to taste because he is partial to it, coming from Yorkshire where they eat a lot. I get some fish, which is said to be excellent brain food but we don't have to buy it because we catch so many trout. I even get the odd bit of salmon. Of course, I could exist on any food which humans like. As the Chap points out, it was our ability to thrive on the same food that originally made the dog–man relationship so easy.

'Bits' are a constant bone of contention between the Chap and the Boss. 'Dogs should not be used as dustbins,' she admonishes, if she spots him slyly passing me a bit of toast or cake or the end of an ice-cream cornet. 'You are nullifying all the exercise you give her,' she bangs on. The Chap replies by arguing that he is simply making use of me in the all-important matter of conservation. He says if I am fed the scraps and allowed to lick plates and pots there will be that much less grease and other pollutants to end up in the rivers via the drains. And, as three fisherfolk, we are, of course, very conscious about the state of the rivers. 'Recycling' he calls it, and every little helps. Of course, I agree with him. Serving as a 'dustbin' is my sacrifice to conservation and I make it willingly. Only humans practice the ludicrous concept of self-denial, which is not in the vocabulary of any self-respecting dog. Though the Boss cannot refute the argument, she thinks that letting dogs lick plates is unhygienic, though she doesn't stop me giving her a loving lick if she is in the mood for fun. Unfortunately, the vets are completely on her side about the bits.

The Chap does not have to be sly at breakfast because we have it alone together while the Boss has hers in bed. On the odd days when she decides to join us I do not do so well. Still, she does save for my bowl what she calls 'delicious left-overs' though if they are so delicious I wonder why are they left over.

Naturally, I watch the Chap, silently but hopefully, when he has something which I think I might share. My most intense concentration is directed at his ice-cream cornet of which it has long been understood that I get the bottom end. The odd thing about a cone is that as the Chap licks it away at the top it still remains a cone but, sadly for me, of diminishing volume. When he is eating a cornet in his usual slow manner I sit myself four-square in front of him and stare at him, fixedly, while still, of course, keeping an eye on the real object of my immediate affection. I know that the pack-leader is entitled to the largest share of the food but two-thirds of a cone is plenty, in this member's opinion. Usually I manage to make him feel guilty if he begins to take more.

The Chap buys two sorts of cornets from the little village sweet shop – giant cones and ordinary. It is a moot point which I prefer. The giant gives me more in the end but I have to wait longer for it. I suspect that such finer points of canine solid geometry have eluded human mathematicians from Pythagoras down the ages.

Another item which runs a cornet close is a jam doughnut. The Chap often gets one from the baker, just up the village street, and even the Boss has accepted that, as his co-author, I am entitled to part of it, including some of the jam. Then there are biscuits. I prefer man biscuits to dog biscuits especially those with chocolate on them. He tells the Boss that anything chocolate must help to keep my chocolate colour going, pointing out that flamingos go pale if they don't get a regular diet of pink shrimps. To this end he doles out a few chocolate drops specially made for dogs in the evening, insisting that it's only natural that a choc dog should like dog chocs. Actually, he is such a chocoholic that I am surprised he isn't chocolate coloured himself.

The Chap's chocolate cupboard, which he restocks at intervals by visits to a wholesaler, contains enough bars, Walnut Whips and Turkish Delights, to withstand a siege. I am particularly partial to part of a Mars Bar because there is a close link in my mind between that and food in general. Pedigree Chum and most of the other dog foods are owned by Mars, the firm that makes the bars. Even better, though, is a dessert called 'Death by Chocolate' served at the local bistro, in Kintbury. My friends, Mark and Jason, who own the bistro, sent me a present of a portion and it was delicious beyond description, soft, sheer, concentrated chocolate. I managed to survive it but what a way to go!

Incidentally, the Chap's chocolate-coloured smoking jacket and trousers, which he usually wears in the evenings, are not really to match me, though they happen to do so. Along with most of his clothes, he had them long before I came on the scene. The Boss's theory is that he likes them because the melted bits that invariably fall off the bar-chocolate he eats in the evening won't show on them. As you can't sponge velvet without leaving a mark, the jacket is now such a mess that the Boss would like him to throw it away but he is too attached to it. What have I said? I don't mean that he can't peel it off, but the Boss hints that it is already getting that way.

On occasion, I am independent for chocolate because fans sometimes send me some to show their appreciation of the pleasure I have brought into their lives. These treats are not under my control but, since the Chap has some chocolate every night after supper, I shame him into giving me some of mine. 'It's all calories,' the Boss complains but he still manages to slip me some, usually when he thinks her eyes are glued to the TV screen. Good Boys are among my favourites even though their name is rather sexist.

A close second to an ice-cream cornet is a marrowbone, which is like a cornet to me because I can get my tongue right into it. I also enjoy chewing on a bone which, to human eyes, seems to be devoid of nutriment. The Chap wonders why I spend quite some time looking at the old dry bones in my toy basket before making a choice, but the question in my mind is the same as the one in his when he is choosing a trout or salmon fly. Which will produce the best result? It's a question of the way his fancy takes him. It's just the same with me. I also enjoy pushing and pursuing a bone about the lawn. Apart from being fun it is a sensible thing to do, especially on a hot day, because a rolling bone gathers no flies. Fortunately, the Boss, who is the one who goes to the butcher, believes that bones are good for my teeth, provided I don't have too many which would wear them down, so they are regularly renewed.

The vets say that eight out of every ten family dogs have tooth trouble and may even suffer from toothache because their teeth are not brushed regularly and they develop stuff called plaque. I suspect that it is partly to get more business and partly a stunt to sell canine toothpaste, which is now being advertised. There is even chicken-flavoured toothpaste to be put on with a 'designer' toothbrush, whatever that may mean. I intend to stick to bones, like my wolf ancestors did, though I also quite like one of those 'chews', which pet shops sell, especially a knobbly one.

All this fuss about food leads the Boss to apply what she calls the pinch test – feeling a fold of my skin to see how loose my coat is, something, I gather, that she does to herself in private. Vets are now organizing 'dog weight-watcher' groups to find the 'canine slimmer of the year' – some nationwide. I have positively no wish to win it but, suddenly, with all the publicity, the Boss decided that I was overweight and should go on a diet and lose 6 pounds, which is more than it seems because it is nearly 10 per cent of my weight. The Chap agreed,

We three
- The Pack

Mike Hollist/Solo Syndication

Making sure that my ghost writer gets it right!

Mike Hollist/Solo Syndication

Signing my book with my pawprint.

Peter Bloodworth

Being welcomed by the manager before opening my bank account at Lloyds.

Lloyds Bank News

At the bank making my first withdrawal.

Jane Wells

Action Stations!

Mike Hollist/Solo Syndication

Relaxing after a shoot.

These save my ears when the gun goes off.

Ian Ross

Alison McGrath

Billee Chapman Pincher

Susan Towers-Clark

Clive Hawes / Evening Standard / Solo Syndication

In the car ready for the off.

Mike Hollist/Solo Syndication

On the River Tay wondering where all the salmon have gone.

Perthshire Advertiser

perhaps feeling guilty about all the titbits he had given me when the Boss wasn't looking, but insisted that it should be under veterinary supervision which made things even worse, to my mind. He seems to have more faith in vets than he has in doctors, from whom he keeps away at all costs. Odd, isn't it, that to vet anything is OK while to doctor anything is suspect.

So, though I felt fine and just couldn't see anything wrong with me, off we went to the dreaded vet, who, that day, was called Mr Blackman, though he is quite white. As soon as we arrived, I disgraced myself by looking apprehensive, meaning that I was shivering and my teeth were chattering so audibly that the Chap said I sounded like an old woodpecker. But, as I will explain later, there were sound reasons for my fear going far back into my puppyhood, which, as any child or pup psychologist will tell you, is the time when unpleasant experiences lead to all kinds of bottled-up anxieties which may appear irrational. My subconscious fear is so deep-seated that I even react to the word 'vet'. So when the Chap and the Boss accuse me of being a coward I don't think that they have sufficient appreciation of the trauma I suffered. And some people say that dogs do not have good memories!

In the waiting-room, where there were other dogs, my efforts to hide behind the Boss's skirts were a little too obvious and caused some comment. The Chap was there, but skirts are better to hide behind than trousers. It was when we went into the surgery – what a terribly suggestive name – that I really got the trembles, especially when Mr Blackman came in in his white coat. I had not met this partner before and he was enormous, which turned out to be a good thing because I had to be weighed and he had no scales. Some bathroom scales were produced and he just picked me up and stood on them. I was so scared that I wet myself. I also wet him slightly so, at least, one life-long ambition was achieved.

Having registered our joint weights, he then put me down and weighed himself, subtracting to get my weight – sixty-six pounds. He then ran a tape-measure over me, which I did not like either, and finally agreed that I ought to lose six pounds, which we already knew. The only good news was that he advised that I should be given six weeks in which to do it. After all, it was like an eleven-stone woman being required to lose a whole stone. I was still against it, however, because it was mid-winter – February – and very cold and I reckoned that I needed that extra weight. My views were ignored but I suppose that one of the penalties for being a famous female is that we have to make sacrifices to stay that way.

The Chap had heard of a new slimming diet, called Pal Lite, composed of big pellets which provide bulk with reduced calories and with the makers' collaboration decided that I should be a guinea-pig – a creature I have never seen. I persevered and the Boss came on a diet with me, not Pal Lite, of course, though the Chap tried it and spat it out. She often diets and then I suffer too because I don't like rabbit food.

As his share, the Chap cut me down to two dog-chocs in the evening and, as a gesture of sympathy, rationed himself to two squares of chocolate, but his self-sacrifice did not last long. It would have been more natural if the whole pack had gone on short commons, as the wolf pack had to when food was short, though even then the pack-leader hogged most of it. The basics of life don't change much, do they?

While I did not complain or beg for more food, I made my feelings felt by pushing round my metal feeding bowl and creating a din with it as soon as it was empty. I suspected that I did not have a dog in hell's chance of getting any more but a dog is entitled to fantasize and the Chap is such a push-over that he might have relented when the Boss wasn't looking. All he said, though, as he took the empty bowl away, was, 'Come on, Dido, there's no taste in nothing,' which was precisely what I was trying to tell him.

He frequently tells me that I should eat to live and not live to eat and that I will live longer if I do not overeat. But bark for yourself, I say. I will always prefer pie on the ground to pie in the sky.

Like him, though, I am interested in having as long a life-span as possible, believing, for reasons I will explain later, that this world is the only one we shall experience and should be enjoyed to the full. To that end I put up with routine visits to the vet for vaccinations against diseases which kill quite a lot of dogs. Fortunately, dogs and humans don't get each other's diseases which, no doubt, has been another reason why both species have managed to get on so well down the centuries. But there is an exception – rabies. I wonder how long before we have to endure routine vaccinations for rabies, which occurs in foxes all over Europe? Right now, the threat may be a cloud no bigger than a dog's paw but with the Channel Tunnel soon opening, some enterprising fox may decide to become an illegal immigrant. Then how long before the caninophobes – the dog-haters – demand that all dogs should be muzzled? I hope it does not happen in my time but I fear it is inevitable.

'In my time?' You should never ask a bitch her age though I have not yet got to the stage where I would be embarrassed to answer – five. Still there are signs. Take my muzzle, for instance. It is not as broad as it was two years ago, rather as the Chap's nose has changed, though that seems even bigger. My ears haven't changed though, while I suspect that the Chap's have actually got bigger as well. Some years ago the artist, John Bratby, painted his portrait and made the ears so big that the Chap wouldn't buy it but I am beginning to think that Bratby was just ahead of his time. I suppose that, because of inexorable ageing changes, none of us, dogs or humans, are really quite the same individual two days running.

In that context, do people come to look like their dogs as they age? Some do because they originally choose a dog that looks like them. They also tend to choose a dog with a similar temperament to their own, aggressive people usually having aggressive dogs, for instance, and this can show up in their facial features. The Chap, though, may be something of an exception. He can be quite aggressive and I am not, though I can look aggressive if I want to. Perhaps he is the same and only looks and sounds aggressive – all wind and water.

Overweight people often have overweight dogs because they indulge their dogs as well as themselves and if they are on a fatty diet their pets get the 'left-overs'. Obesity tends to obliterate features so they can begin to look a bit alike in that respect. With ageing, the skin sags in both species and we both develop jowls. Regular smiling changes the features and if an owner and his dog are smilers they might become more alike on that score, so long as they both have plenty to smile about, as the Chap and I have. Anyway, if the Chap and the Boss end up looking like me they won't do too badly.

While most humans care what their dogs look like we don't care what they look like – handsome is as handsome does – but, with our extremely sensitive noses, we may care what they smell like. Do people come to smell like their dogs? The Chap wants to know. It is undeniable that some old dogs can become odorous, though washing and spraying can usually neutralize that, but, as my nose is so much more sensitive than the Chap's, he should put up with my scent when I have endured his without complaint for so long.

There is one ageing sign of which I am increasingly aware. Some days I awaken as full of beans as my beanbag; on others I don't want to get up and I indulge in a long lie-in, even declining the morning invitation to accompany the Chap upstairs when he comes down to pick up the papers at about 7 a.m. However, I still *look* the same first thing in the morning as I do during the day which is more than you can say for most human females. The Chap says that some of them are unrecognizable without their war-paint, of which I have no need, though I confess that there have been odd occasions, prior to a photo-call, when the Boss has covered up the odd temporary blemish on my face with her eyebrow pencil.

My coat is still glossy and loose, like a puppy's, my teeth remain excellent, my vision superb, and most of the time I'm raring to go. A bitch is as old as she feels and, by and large, I feel great. I did get a shock though, recently, when my feathered pal, George, the canary, had a stroke and died. I always thought that a stroke was something nice and to be welcomed. But there was George, looking in great nick after his moult and singing his heart out. Then in two days he was gone, in spite of every effort to revive him. Life hangs by a thread and just as many dogs seem to be cut off in their prime as humans. But I don't intend to spend much time thinking about that. I've proved that I am an achiever. Now I need to prove that I am a survivor. In these hazardous times that will be an achievement in itself.

117

10 Family Secrets

Then what can birth on mortal dogs bestow?

My former mistress, Alison, bought me when a litter of seven chocolate Labradors was advertised in *Horse and Hound* magazine. Alison, who worked as a hunt groom at East Kennet, induced a friend to drive her down to Devon and she returned with a bitch puppy, named at the Kennel Club as Keneven Fantasy and then six weeks old. That was me! Or should I say 'I'? Obviously she had to find a handier name and, looking through one of her mother's books on mythology, she came across the name Dido and settled for it. Dido was the famous Queen who founded Carthage and had a lover called Aeneas. I am proud to bear her name, not only because she was regal but because she was a smart cookie. When she emigrated to Africa she easily obtained a grant of land from the local ruler because she asked only for enough as could be covered by an ox-hide. She then cut the hide into thousands of strips so narrow that when she tied them all together they encircled enough land to build a big city. I like to think that I would have been as astute but the ruler could not have been very clever with the small print.

It looks as though Dido also had a dog because, when visiting the Vatican, the Chap saw a 1500-year-old parchment book about her and Aeneas with coloured pictures showing dogs. One of them had a fine, royal-looking collar but it was a Dalmatian, no doubt because Labradors were not then available.

Of course, Alison was given my pedigree form which means that I can trace my ancestry back through more generations than most people can. It is on record further back still at the Kennel Club. How many humans can claim that they are thoroughbreds, as I, undoubtedly, can? I suspect that a lot of you would have to be classed as mutts, though, of course, all blood, however mongrel, is of ancient origin.

From my birth I have been very much a country dog, enjoying life around horses, sheep and lots of pheasants. I understand that I was taught not to chase pheasants or partridges but I fear that I soon forgot those lessons. There was one lesson I did not forget, however. When I was only eight weeks old I swallowed a bumble-bee and was stung in the throat so badly that my whole face swelled up so that I could not see. That led to my first encounter with a vet and I did not like it though, no doubt, he was doing his best for me because I could have died from being unable to breathe. I must have been somewhat accident-prone as a pup because, after the bumble-bee crisis, when I was six months old, I damaged the stifle on my back leg through an unfortunate contact with a horse. I had to undergo an operation, which so intensified my fear of vets that the mere scent of the surgery gives me the jitters. As I was heavily bandaged for quite a while I had to pay several visits to the surgery and understand that the vet muzzled me during his various operations, presumably because I gave him a nip. He must have done a great job, though, because, after the wound healed, I never experienced any further trouble.

Once Alison had decided to emigrate my future was totally at stake because she decided that she did not wish to take me with her in case she did not like it for, if she came back, I would have to be in quarantine for six months and she knew that I would not only hate that but might pine away for lack of affection. So there was nothing for it but to find a good home for me. A farmer wanted me, and I might easily have gone to him, which would certainly have pre-empted any literary career, but by great, good fortune (for me, anyway) Alison heard of a couple who were deeply distressed, having just lost two old dogs through age and illness, and were seeking a replacement to fill the void.

I have told the story of how I entered the lives of the Chap and the Boss in my first book, but the circumstances which caused us all to fall in love at first sniff and first sight are, perhaps, worth repeating, briefly, as being possibly unique in the annals of dogdom. The Chap was recording an interview about spies for ITN, the television news service, when Alison knocked on the door to present me. By remarkable coincidence, the crew happened to need a dog for a shot of the Chap walking through the churchyard next to the house, and I obliged before he had bought me or even taken a close look. A couple of hours later we appeared on TV together so, clearly, we had been destined for each other. However, once they had taken a closer look, they could not wait to part with their money and seal the purchase, though they had never owned a Labrador before. The Chap says it was the best deal he ever made and I agree with him. My arrival was what he calls a 'mutation moment' – one of those chance events which condition the lives of all of us. Whatever it did for mine, I certainly mutated his life for him! Before I arrived AD meant Anno Domini. I leave you to guess what it means now.

The new members of my pack were aware that I would suffer some psychological trauma from the parting from Alison and went out of their way to make me welcome. In fact, there was such a nice niche waiting that I slipped into it without any trouble at all and found my paws in two minutes flat. Even the doormat had a silhouette of a Labrador on it which seemed another prophetic coincidence. However, as I was to learn later, things are never quite what they seem in the human world. The Chap had really gone out to buy a doormat with the words 'Beware of the Wife' on it but the shop had sold out and the Labrador mat was his frustration buy.

Being attracted by what she had read about Australia, Alison went there and secured a job on a cattle stud called Thologolong, where Murray grey cattle are bred. She has written to tell me how she fell in love with the next-door neighbour, Des McGrath, and married him. He is a grazier who runs Angus cattle and Merino sheep on 5,000 acres on the banks of the mighty Murray River in the state of Victoria. She, too, has now given birth and has also acquired another dog but it is a Beagle (like Snoopy) because she decided that she could never have a Labrador after me as I was the best that anyone could wish to have and none other could compare. Whether true or not, it was a wonderful compliment.

My fame has put me in touch with some of my family who wrote after reading about me or seeing me on television and they were all kind enough to say how proud they are of me. My mother, Tarka, so-called because, like me, she has a tail like an otter, was the first to write (at least the letter was signed by her). She was glad to hear that all her efforts on my education had not been wasted. 'Keep your man under your little paw, as we have tried to teach you,' she advised. 'They are not much good on their own,' with which, of course, I agree. Like me, Mum is full of life and enthusiasm. She reminded me that I had three brothers and three sisters and her letter was accompanied by a colour photograph of us all lined up at our bowls. There was not a runt among us, so Mother Tarka had done us proud.

I then received a long letter from my long-lost father, whose name I knew as Kerswell Copper King but who turned out to be generally called Wellington. Writing from the village of Abbotskerswell, near Newton Abbot in Devon, and addressing me as 'My dearest daughter, Dido,' he was delighted with my success and was able to tell me that, at the age of ten, he is fit and well and that his mother, my grandma, another chocolate dog called Brandy, is also alive. There are a number of younger Labradors at the kennels there and they help to keep Dad and Grandma young. Like me, my father is a keen water dog and prefers to swim along the local river rather than walk the bank. Apparently, when Dad was young, his owners received a huge offer for him from some Americans but they turned it down flat which was great for me because if he had emigrated I wouldn't have been born, would I? Dad wants me to keep in touch with him and I shall certainly do that, exchanging photographs and so on.

I also heard from an uncle, my father's brother, who is called Napoleon, and a brother called Winston. (You see, most of us happen to be named after famous people.) Most of my relatives sent colour pictures, having seen mine in the *Daily Mail*. I must say, we do all look alike! The pictures form quite a collection for me to look at, perhaps, when I am old and retired from writing though, if I am like the Chap, I will never do that.

The Chap was specially delighted to find that, like his ancestors, some of mine, including my grandma, Brandy, came from Yorkshire, not far from where he spent, or mis-spent, his youth. I think that mine were more distinguished than his, achieving fame in the show ring. Indeed, my great great grandmother was the famous Cookridge Tango, the first British chocolate to become a Champion Labrador.

I thought that, with such a background, I had better join the Labrador Retrievers Club which I did in 1991 when it celebrated its seventy-fifth year. Naturally, the Queen is the Club's patron.

So far as my really distant ancestry is concerned, nobody has yet written *The Descent of Dog* – the book Darwin should have written, with all the details of Neanderthal Dog, Piltdown Dog, Dawn Dog and such like. We know, of course, that way back in prehistoric time we descended from wolves so I am, to some extent, a wolf in dog's clothing. Come to think of it, I can trace my ancestry right back to the wolf, while your ancestry is lost in the mists of prehistoric man. There are theories about the creature you are descended from but no proof, though the odds are that it was something like an ape. Perhaps the Chap will write the book one day though, with the way things are looking in my neck of the woods, perhaps it should be called *The Ascent of Dog*.

11 Dido the Water Dog

*Oh Kennet banks are fair and wide with lots of reeds
    and tufts,
I'd rather roam with my Chap there than reign the
    Queen of Cruft's*

There is no place I like better than being on a river bank
helping the Chap or the Boss to catch fish and generally
mooching around. Every time I find myself there I bless
the old commercial fishermen of Newfoundland who
generated my breed to assist them in their tough life
catching cod in the rough Atlantic waters. Our thick
coats enabled us to swim in the coldest sea and retrieve
the cod which fell off the hooks as the long lines
were being hauled into the small boats. We would also
swim between boats carrying ropes and retrieve small
objects swept off the decks. It was while watching a
display of this ability from a boat in Poole Harbour,
which had been delivering salted cod, that a former
Earl of Malmesbury realized that Labradors, as we
became known, might retrieve wildfowl which fell into
water when shot. He acquired a breeding stock and
now I and my kind are the commonest – and best –
retrievers in the shooting field, able to sit in the cold
and rain without discomfort. We Labradors are not
just fair-weather friends. We have a built-in all-weather
capability, as the scientists say.

We still retain our fishing instincts. At least, I do. It is so deep in our genes that I never fail to get excited when the Chap or the Boss hooks a fish and, to be honest, I am as fanatical about fishing as the Chap is, and that's saying something. I can tell by the screech of the reel when it is a fish and not just the Chap reeling in or pulling off the line. I know where he is likely to land it and position myself there. I would love to land the fish by mouth but the Chap was diffident about letting me try in case I got the hook in my mouth or my eye. Then, after reading about me in *Country* magazine, for which the Chap writes on fishing, I received a letter from a seven-year-old black Labrador, called Brig, who wrote with instructions, saying that the Chap did not have enough faith in me. He told me to land the fish by the head. So the Chap decided to have the courage and let me try with a two-pound trout that was played out. I can't say that I made a clean job of my first attempt but we got it out and there was not a tooth mark on it. The legendary softness of our mouths is one of the major reasons why most of us are such good gun dogs.

Normally, I am allowed to lick the fish's gills once it has been knocked on the head. My tongue has become adept at turning back the gill covers and, though I may be the first dog to discover that, whatever it is that is on the gills of a freshly caught trout or salmon is quite delicious. Out of curiosity, because the Chap, a frustrated scientist, wants to know everything first hand, he licked the gills of a fresh fish himself – there's no end to his eccentricities. I watched his face as he did it. Quite clearly he could not taste anything at all so trout-gill licks are for the canine connoisseur only. I suspect my tongue is much more sensitive than his.

To celebrate my landing my first fish I did not get the ritual 'dram' of whisky – the Chap gave up all alcohol years ago – but a bit of a jam-filled doughnut he had in his pocket for 'elevenses'. I appreciated that for him to share his riverside doughnut was quite a sacrifice, though I did not get any of the jammy bits. Since then he has let me land several other trout and I have not muffed one yet. Now, when my Chap hooks a fish it's all paws to the pumps, as it is when he, or anyone else, falls in, though how long we will be able to continue either to fish or fall in is in doubt. So much water is being abstracted from the Kennet, its tributaries and the bore-holes that feed them, to assuage the domestic and industrial thirst of Swindon that the river gets lower every year. Marlborough, only a few miles upstream, is already seriously affected and there are many parts of our stretch which became too shallow to hold fish.

While I am prepared to be the Chap's assistant on the river, because in the study he is mine, what I would really like to do is to catch a fish entirely on my own and I have made a few stabs at it, in one particular place, though so far without success. However, like all anglers, I live in hope and I still think I'm in with a good chance with what the Chap calls 'Dido's Game'. When we fish up a small offshoot of the River Kennet (called a carrier) we come to a little wooden bridge over a narrow and shallow outlet from one of the fish ponds in which Peter, the keeper, rears his rainbow trout. These fish are fed on brown food-pellets and, as they float, a few of them drift into the outlet. Each year there are one or two trout living in the carrier who spot these pellets and wait for them, moving up a few yards into the outlet and above the little wooden bridge over it.

The Chap has tried stalking them in the hope of putting a tempting fly over them but, so far, they have always spotted him and raced down under the bridge out of the outlet back into the carrier. The more promising possibilities for me did not escape my notice for long. As soon as we get to the little bridge I get down, very quietly, into the water below it and wait for the fish to race down. Then I have a go at them. This is what wolves must have done, and maybe still do, to catch the salmon moving in the smaller streams in Canada. The trout are usually quite large – at least three pounds – but, so far, I have never managed to get one, though I have been, literally, within a whisker of doing so.

It is, of course, a very difficult goal because I have to try to catch them with my mouth and they are very fast. But never mind! The difficulty only increases the challenge – and the fun – and I am sure that I will succeed eventually as experience improves my skill. Even if I never succeed it beats Pooh sticks any day!

In spite of my failure to score I have managed to impress the Chap with one aspect of 'Dido's Game'. It was last season that I cottoned on to it and the Chap wondered whether I would remember it this year, after a gap of eight months. I did, with no trouble at all. The moment I spotted the bridge I was in and under it, though I missed the fish again. Like all fishers I am patient and I'll get one one day.

Being permitted to go under the bridge is a dispensation because I'm supposed to be pegged down all the time I'm on the river. The Chap does this using a big corkscrew tether made for goats, which gives the other fishermen a laugh when they see it. There is only one place where the Chap wades and that's at the bottom of a deep stream called the Pumphouse Pool. He always makes sure that I'm well pegged down there because I might follow him in and there are pike in it longer than me.

I have one other, possibly unique, fishing function. On our water we have to return any trout which are less than fourteen inches long, but have to take any which are that length or longer. The Chap has a fourteen-inch measure marked out on the handle of his net but if that is not handy he has an alternative. He measured my tail at exactly eleven inches long, so by laying a trout alongside it he can easily see if it is undersize. Sweet are the uses of an extremity! And what a good thing that my tail was not docked when I was a pup! For a dog, being without a tail is like being deprived of your fingers. How would you feel if you couldn't put even two fingers up? And how would Italians and some other nationalities communicate if their hands were docked at birth? A tail is our built-in signalling system and a dog without a tail is made partly dumb. Its purposes are, in fact, dogifold, being important for balance, turning and braking. Yet, for many years, the tails of breeds like the Boxer, the Poodle, the Spaniel and the Corgi were cut off to conform with fashion or some crackpot belief. Happily, from July 1993, it has become illegal for anyone but vets to remove any part of a dog's tail, except when they believe that it is necessary for a medical reason – one aspect of canine law with which I am in absolute agreement. Further, vets have been warned that they risk being struck off if they dock a tail for purely cosmetic purposes. In fact, I called for an end to docking in my first book, so perhaps I had a small paw in the campaign. Some gun dog owners are still arguing that Spaniels will damage their tails in thick cover and pick up dirt and brambles if they are not docked. This is nonsense. I don't damage my tail and I get into thick cover at shoots and by the waterside. Foxhounds, too, are never docked.

A few breeds, especially the Corgi and the Boxer, are going to look strange at first with their tails of the unexpected, but will be all the more handsome for being more natural. I just feel sorry for all those already-docked dogs who cannot fully express their appreciation of the good news.

We go down to the river quite a lot for spells of a couple of hours, usually just the Chap and me, so much, in fact, that the Boss says we will both end up growing fins. If someone telephones the Chap when the 'Gone fishin' ' notice is on his desk the Boss quips, 'He's down on the river with his nymph.' This intrigues non-fishers and she has to explain that the nymph isn't a young woman (whoever heard of an old nymph?) or even me. It's a kind of trout fly.

It is not just the fishing that I love. It's the whole environment. Apart from the running water, which I like for its own sake, there are reeds and tufts of flowers to nose into, coots, moorhens, ducks and voles to spook. A vole is my favourite because I can smell it in its burrow, stalk it silently, choosing the precise moment for my pounce with great care, sometimes standing motionless with one paw in the air for half a minute. I never fail to be astonished when I fail to connect and hear a plop into the water but, as with so many things in life, the anticipation is more than half the pleasure.

While the Chap discourages me, there are times when I can't avoid putting up a pheasant or two because there are so many of them. Though I meet other dogs on the river, such as Monty, the *Shooting Times* Springer Spaniel, I used to be the only chocolate dog there, but my monopoly has been broken by another Labrador, called Truffle because he is a much lighter colour than me. This has its advantages for if the estate shooting keeper gets a false report that a chocolate dog has been rampaging around it does not necessarily have to be me any more.

Sometimes we disturb a big roe deer drinking, and on such occasions the Chap waxes lyrical about what he calls his 'Pastoral Symphony' – the harmony of his whole country life which has given him such pleasure. My friend, Peter, the river keeper on the Kennet, once showed me a big Buddleia bush covered with so many peacock butterflies that when the Chap shook the branches scores fluttered off and then resettled, but I wasn't able to catch one of them. On the Dee, in Scotland, where we fish, I nosed out a stone under a hut where otters leave their deposits. A rare aroma indeed and one for my collection of smell memories!

I sometimes find tennis balls which occasionally float down the Kennet and in Scotland I have pulled out golf balls. The Chap used to bang on about his old Springer Spaniel who had such a soft mouth that she would find hens' eggs in the orchard and bring them in without a mark on them. Mercifully, I have heard no more of that since I pulled a Canada Goose's egg out of the Kennet and presented it to him without a tooth mark to be seen. He was most impressed.

I have had to become something of a bird-watcher because there are some black swans on the Kennet which have escaped from another estate and, I suppose, are coloured immigrants, like my ancestors were. They are rather aggressive but I'm not going to be told off or seen off by Aussies. No way! I let them see who's tougher. The white swans are a different proposition though, because they are much bigger and stronger, so I have learned not to go near their nests and we have established a *modus vivendi*.

Being a bitch I do not have the male dog's particular interest in trees but the Chap is dotty about them.

As a former botanist and conserver he is invariably infuriated when he sees or hears a lovely tree being cut down, especially now that trees are so important for absorbing and storing the excessive amounts of carbon dioxide being pumped into the air by industry and motor cars, with all the damage it is doing to the ozone layer. 'Never send to know for whom the chain-saw whines; It whines for thee!' he declares. Of course, when trees are burned to clear land he gets more furious because the tons of carbon dioxide safely locked up in them is set free immediately to do its damage. The trees also produce vast amounts of the oxygen we need, so when you kill them you are effectively reducing the size of the earth's lungs. Still, so many of you ruin your own lungs with tobacco smoke that I don't suppose that will worry you.

A special joy for me on our stretch of the Kennet is finding those savoury brown pellets on which my friend Peter, the river keeper feeds his fish. There are usually a few dropped, accidentally, round the stew-ponds where he rears his brown and rainbow trout and even on the river bank in certain places where he gives the fish a bit of extra nourishment early in the season if natural food is scarce. I find them very tasty but my best find was when I was taken to the Berkshire Trout Farm which is owned by one of the Chap's shooting pals. Located near Hungerford, it was one of the first trout farms in Britain – the ponds having been dug by the navvies who dug the Kennet and Avon Canal which runs close by. And I do mean dug – by spades and barrows. I am something of a digger myself – when I accidentally root out one of his plants the Chap calls me 'the dirty digger' – but I stand in awe when I see the whole length of that canal and realize it was all dug by human hand.

The farm started producing trout for stocking rivers in 1906 – even before the old Chap was born – and now turns out two million a year, all for stocking trout rivers and lakes. They eat tons of pellets and, on my tour, I was delighted to find many of them lost in the grass round the ponds. I was fascinated to see so many fish but was even more interested in the pellets.

What fascinated the Chap was to see birds like robins and wagtails raiding the long trays holding the trout eggs and the just-hatched babies. Who would have thought it of a robin? The blackbirds are so much worse that the owner had put up a dummy owl in the shed with the egg trays. All I can say is that it didn't scare the robins. Still, with ten million eggs being hatched out each year there are plenty left. The Chap says that when he was a boy there was a song – 'Three seeds in a hole – one for the crow, one to rot and one to grow'. So fish farmers don't do so badly, though once the baby trout are put into the ponds outside, the ducks and moorhens decimate them, as they do in the wild, only more so. Later it is the kingfishers and herons which raid them. I can see that it is hard for fish farmers to be bird lovers when they see their profits flying away.

I should point out that while I always get excited when the Chap has hooked a good fish I never bark about it when we are on a trout river but I always do when he hooks a salmon. I don't know exactly why I do this but the Chap encourages me because it serves a most useful purpose. When my couple are on a salmon river they are usually some distance apart in different pools and often out of sight of each other. As there is usually only one gillie the Chap always ensures that he is with the Boss in case she gets her bait caught on the bottom of the river (though I suspect it is because he knows she is more likely to hook a salmon). If I bark the gillie is likely to come down to see what is happening and be on hand in case the Chap is into a whopper. Maybe, because we are so close, his sense of excitement is transmitted to me. This has occurred more than once. Fish cannot hear aerial sounds so it doesn't matter if I bark or even burst into song, like it does if we are out shooting.

Apparently Brig, the black Labrador who wrote to me, even lands salmon but I doubt, with salmon so scarce, that the Chap would let me tackle one. The Chap says that the take of a salmon is the most exciting experience which life has to offer (not very complimentary to the Boss, I feel), so I can't see him allowing me to interfere with that in any way. Brig also told me not to let my Chap ever use two flies at once on a cast, as some fishermen do, especially for salmon, because when he was landing a fish which was hooked on the top fly the lower fly got hooked in his rear end. Perhaps that's why anglers call that fly the tail fly!

There is no sport where the unexpected is encountered so often or in such variety as fishing. So much so that the Boss has collected two volumes of true fishing stories which are stranger than any fiction. She is calling the second one *Tails and the Unexpected*, which shows that I am not the only member of the pack guilty of punning.

I particularly love salmon fishing because we are in such wild places that I am allowed to roam along the banks which are usually riddled with rabbit holes. Also when the Chap is wading he usually allows me to get into the water up to my belly so I feel really part of the action. I can't do that on the trout river which is too small for any unnecessary disturbance. I get an extra laugh when he goes over the top of his big salmon waders going just that bit further in and has to come out

133

to empty them, when I hear a few new English words.

One thing we are very careful about on the river bank is to leave no bits of nylon cast there, cutting it up into very small pieces that can do no harm. Once, when we were fishing on the Dee in Scotland, we came across a beautiful bird which excited the Chap when he recognized it as a fulmar petrel. Seeing that there must be something wrong with it from the way it was sitting the Chap went to pick it up but unfortunately it flew away revealing yards of tangled nylon round its legs. It could neither walk nor swim and was destined to starve unless, as we hoped, someone could catch it and release it. In spite of the Chap's precautions, he made a blunder in the garden leaving a strand about eight inches long on the ground and forgetting to cut it up. A blackbird incorporated it into its nest in such a way that it left a loop about two inches long sticking out. Sadly, the female caught her head in it and strangled herself after she had laid five eggs.

Last year on the Tay, at Kinnaird, I experienced a new aspect of fishing which also dates back to my origins. On the beat which we were allotted a lot of the fishing is done from boats and I had never realized before what fun boats can be. I was a bit diffident at first about getting in every morning but soon they couldn't keep me out of it. You get quite a different view of the river and there is great excitement when someone hooks a fish from the boat. Not quite like old times off Newfoundland but a taste of it.

Some of the other fishermen were using worms which are not only allowed for salmon but used to be fished regularly by the Queen Mum at Balmoral, according to a reliable Deeside gillie friend of mine. The Chap doesn't like using them but told the worm-fishers a tale about his boyhood days when he used them to catch trout in the river Tees. He once forgot about some worms he had in a tin in moist sphagnum moss and his mother found it and opened it weeks later. The smell was the worst she had ever experienced – too appalling, I gather, even for a dog. So far as his mother was concerned, this *sphagnum opus*, as he recalled it, was the last time he brought worms into the house. Perhaps this was the origin of that phrase I hear so often – a 'can of worms', which is something that everyone avoids opening.

Perhaps, one day, the Chap will take me sea-fishing. That would be even more nostalgic. I have been to the sea a few times and get letters from fans who live there. One of them, a yellow Labrador called Chips, spends his spare time immersed in the sea digging out stones which he arranges in a heap on the sand. The fact that he likes being immersed in the briny could well be a throw-back to his origins as a fishing dog in Newfoundland. The stones could be a substitute for the fish which were retrieved and, perhaps, the Labradors were originally trained by the fishermen to put all the fish they secured into a heap, though it is more likely that they were delivered singly to hand. All dogs have their idiosyncracies and it may be that Chips just likes making pyramids like children like making sandcastles.

You will understand, now, why I am always loath to leave any river bank, coming in slowly and reluctantly when I realize that the Chap is putting his rod in the car, or I might even hide behind the hut, if that is where we are, to prolong the enjoyment. I want to savour all aspects of fishing and would like to be remembered as a great fishing dog which is something much rarer and more special than a great gun dog.

It is true that all good things, like the fishing season, come to an end, and I was very sad to miss the last couple of days of the 1992 season through being imminent with pups, though the Chap had the grace to say that it was not the same on the river without me. What I fear is that with some rivers, including my beloved Kennet, fishing there may come to a total end because, as I have mentioned, so much water is being increasingly abstracted for domestic and industrial purposes that the flow is drying up, in spite of the odd wet winter. As some poet almost wrote about a stream, 'Dogs may come and dogs may go but I go on for ever'. That is no longer true. Some streams near us have been sucked completely dry and may never run regularly again. Tragedy!

12 Farewell to Arms

All good things come to an end

Towards the end of that hot August in 1990 there was mounting excitement because we were all going to some North Yorkshire moors to shoot grouse. The moors, in two valleys called Teesdale and Swaledale, were near where the Chap had spent his boyhood. In those days he used to visit them on his bike and he has been in love with them ever since. It was there, as I have heard him tell many times, that he was assaulted by a grouse in a way which left a permanent mark on his already craggy features.

When he was in his fifties he was in a butt when a covey of grouse suddenly appeared in front of him, travelling with the wind at something like forty miles an hour. He shot one dead and was about to fire at a second when he was struck in the face by what felt like a cricket bat. It was the dead grouse which, hurtling on, had struck him plumb on his outsize nose, breaking it and blacking both his eyes. He claimed that he shed more blood that day than all the grouse shot in Yorkshire. His dog, a Springer called Scoop, witnessed it and though, no doubt, concerned, must have smiled at the poetic justice of it all. I do wish that I had seen it. I am sure I would not have been able to resist the equivalent of a canine guffaw.

Sadly, a couple of weeks before we were due on the moor, there was such a shortage of grouse, owing to some awful disease, that shooting had to be cancelled. Still we did go up just for a social weekend and I really enjoyed myself when we all went for a picnic on Reeth Moor with a lot of nice new friends, including several dogs. Dry heather is marvellous stuff to bounce around in and I put up a cock grouse which made a noise just like, 'Go back, go back!' I also found that I could run up and down slopes so nearly vertical that the Boss was really worried for me. The only thing I didn't like much was the taste of the water which had collected on the peat, though the stream water was nice.

The whole moor was littered with the remnants of ancient, abandoned lead mines with shafts and caverns which present some danger to the over-adventurous dog sent to recover a grouse. I heard lots of tales about dogs which had gone down there and never been seen again, though some had turned up days later when, being thinner through starvation, they could squeeze through narrow gaps.

On our way back the Chap made the gloomy pronouncement that he had shot his last grouse because he thought that his chances of being invited again at his age were remote, grouse shooting being for younger people who are faster on the trigger. As it turned out his prediction was true. In fact, after only one more season, he decided to retire from shooting altogether – after forty years of letting his gun off at some of the best shoots in the land and I am afraid that I was partly responsible for that.

I have described in my first book how I was nearly two years old when I acquired the Boss and had never been trained as a gun dog. Nevertheless, because I came from good working stock, the Chap had high hopes that I would still make one and took me to a lot of famous shoots where, for the most part, people were understanding about my lack of expertise, though a few referred to me as 'that raging hound' when I was let off my lead at the end of a big drive and raced round inspecting the birds that everyone had shot instead of bringing back the Chap's. My mounting excitement at seeing the pheasants and partridges come over signalled the end of my shooting career. I could not resist a yelp to let the Chap know they were on the way and this went down badly with the other guns who imagined that it might stop the birds from coming. In fact, there was more than one occasion when I was of service to the owner because he was able to blame me when few pheasants came when, in truth, there just weren't many there. I don't like being a fall-dog, which is an all too common canine predicament in the shooting field. Time and again, in my brief field career, I have seen dogs berated, or worse, because their owners were shooting badly.

Two gun dog trainers offered to take me for a couple of months to correct my faults but the Chap could not bear to be parted from me for so long.

My last appearance 'at the peg' – where the Chap stood to shoot – was at Wintershall, one of our favourite shoots in a lovely part of Surrey. We were all lined up by one of the duckponds and as the mallards kept coming round and round, very high, it became altogether too exciting to keep quiet. The Labrador at the next peg joined in, and soon we were in full song, to the great annoyance of his owner. I was afraid that he might get a wallop, for which I would have been responsible, but his master stayed his hand. Nevertheless, what became known as the Duckpond Duet convinced the Chap that if he was to have any hope of being asked to shoot again, I should not be.

He continued to take me to shoots but kept me in the car, only letting me out at the end of each drive. I fear that I ruined that final privilege by chewing through one of the seat-belts – an expensive tantrum because the whole equipment had to be replaced, gravity ball and all. We all have our idiosyncracies and, when I feel really frustrated, mine is chewing seat-belts.

Eventually, there was only one solution – I was left at home. Served me right, I suppose. If I had made the grade as a gun dog he might have continued to shoot for my sake. I didn't like being left behind so, when he finally told the Boss 'I've decided to give it up', he took the bark right out of my mouth. It was all for the best, really. He was getting slow with his gun and doing his nut every time he missed an easy bird or drew a bad peg-number, which could not have been good for his blood pressure. Further, it had all become too expensive, even with his share of the royalties from my first book.

It was sad for me, I suppose, though now that he does not go shooting I do not get left behind and we go on walks where I can make as much noise as I like. What I liked most about shooting was the places to which it took us, especially when we stayed the night, like Braxted Park in Essex, for instance. Incidentally, regarding all this talk about 'Essex man' and 'Essex girl', I couldn't see any difference. As for 'Essex dog', those I encountered looked no different either.

There will be many shooting friends whom we are

unlikely to meet again but the Chap has taken it all very well, saying that he has had a marvellous run and the time had come anyway. But I suspect that, beneath that nonchalant exterior, he misses it all very much. I felt his sadness, particularly, on the day that we took his trusty pair of guns to the sale-room, which really did mark the end of his shooting career. These old friends, which had given him so much pleasure, had been made in the 1930s by a man called Henry Atkin, who had been a senior gunmaker with the great firm of Purdey and then set up on his own. Fittingly, it was a grey, rainy day and I could sense that the old Chap was in the dumps and that he was trying not to show it. He always hides his feelings but I can see through him. It was a poignant farewell to arms. No more days in the line with the high and the mighty, the rich and the famous. The end of an era for him.

This was quickly followed by the trauma of having to decline invitations to places like Broadlands, Highclere, Faccombe, Rothwell, Ripley and Wintershall. His friends did all they could to induce him to change his mind and even offered to lend him a gun but, having taken the decision, there could be no going back. As with any addiction, abstinence has to be total or he would slide back, with all the withdrawal symptoms being repeated.

Happily he has cheered up now and behaves as though he is not giving it a thought when he hears them all banging away round our village, which is surrounded by shoots. To let the dog out of the bag, I don't really give a growl myself so long as he does not give up fishing and he has promised me that he will never do that as long as he can drag himself down to the river. As he put it, he could give up shooting with equanimity but, if he gave up fishing, it would probably signify that he was tired of life. He may even take up pike-fishing again in the winter. Learning to do nothing would be every bit as difficult for me as it would be for the Chap.

13 Love Me, Love My Man (and his Wife)

The lonely of heart is withered away

An authoress who intends to go on authoring must stay in close touch with her ghost and I certainly do that with the Chap. After all, I am his dogspiration and except for our sleeping hours and the increasingly rare occasions when he goes to London we are together. I make a point of keeping him in view at all times to ensure that he does not slope off without me. Humans say, 'Out of sight, out of mind.' I think, 'Out of sight! Where the hell is he?'

My first sight of him in the morning is when he comes down for the newspapers. I have usually been waiting for an excuse to bark both of my minders awake and that comes when the papers are stuffed through the letter-box at about 7 a.m. Before he descends he puts a net cover on the bed. When he takes me upstairs I know that I mustn't jump up until they are both back in bed otherwise he can't get in because I sprawl. The Boss says there are some days when I look very long and on all days I am very heavy on the legs – their legs. Serious dog trainers say that it is a mistake to allow a dog on the bed, or on any piece of furniture, because humans should maintain the advantage of their height to help them assert their superiority. Our pack is maintained by mutual trust and love, not by superiority or fear. Also, the Chap says that, at his time of life, it is easier for him if I come up to his level on occasion than for him to come down to mine, though he still makes that effort.

Depending on my mood and how much attention I am being given I may stay on the bed for a few minutes or even half an hour. They delay opening the papers to give me my morning greeting but the Chap can't wait long before opening his paper – with his left hand because his right hand is busy tickling my chest. He starts near the back of the paper because one of the first things he looks at each morning is the obituary columns. I sense that noting the death of someone younger than himself seems to give him a peculiar satisfaction, as though it were a little victory over the hazards that threaten survival, his main concern these days. I can almost hear him saying, 'Ah well, I've seen him out!' as though it were some sort of achievement, as I suppose it is for someone who regards his main job, these days, as avoiding the ultimate job – pushing up daisies.

Once they start to read the papers with both hands I'm off. All I want to do then is to get down into the hall and sit, contentedly, in the little patch of sunlight which usually shines through the fanlight over the door. Sunshine is linked with happiness so it's a bad start to the day when there isn't a patch, though I lie where I think one will come. With his usual wit, the Chap says I do it to get brown, like girls mop up every moment of sunshine. Very funny!

Inevitably, when he comes down he pats me and, while I always appreciate affection, I make it clear that all I want him to do is to get out of my sunlit patch. He retaliates by calling me Diogenes because an ancient

144

Greek philosopher of that name, who lived like a dog in a tub, did the same to Alexander the Great. When Alexander offered him anything he might wish he just asked the great commander to get out of his light. I can see exactly what he meant. Alexander is supposed to have been so impressed that he said, 'If I were not Alexander I would be Diogenes.' I haven't heard the Chap say he would be Dido but he might well think it. On reflection, he might make quite a good dog.

The post usually arrives while we are having our breakfast *à deux*, having taken the Boss's upstairs on a tray, and I get my second bark of the morning. As the postman knows, it is a bark of welcome and he is in no danger if we have to open the door. During the so-called 'Savage Dogs Crisis', which resulted in a ban on four breeds of 'killer' dogs, the hullabaloo rubbed off so unfairly on us law-abiding dogs that the Post Office took to printing a notice on letters – 'Please control your dog when the postman calls' – as though I would harm the man who brings me fan mail and treats!

The post decides the Chap's mood for a while. When it's all bills the outlook is bleak but he brightens if there is a cheque in it, saying that any day which starts with a cheque, however small, can't be too bad. There is another mood-determining breakfast event on certain days, though – when he cuts the top off his boiled egg. He gets rattled if any yolk runs down the shell when he cuts the top off, saying that it is a bad omen for the day. If he really believes that it is his only superstition.

From breakfast on, I keep him in view except for my spell alone on the lawn, if it is a bone day, and a quiet afternoon dog-nap, laid my length on the back seat of my estate car if the weather is very hot. The seat exactly fits my outstretched length with my head on what he calls the arm rest but is really a head rest. Most of the time, though, we are in the study where, without me, he would have nothing to talk to but his word processor. They also serve who only lie and wait. I even barge into his bathroom when I know he is there or hear the electric shaver going if he hasn't shut the door properly and scrape outside if he has. Sometimes I catch him trying to save his precious time by doing two chores at once. He is not embarrassed, recalling that Louis XIV did everything in public, including sitting on his commode. Apparently, there was intense competition among the high-ranking courtiers for the honour of what was called 'holding the cotton'. Include me out!

I also try to keep tabs on the Boss, though she won't permit intrusions like that. So we form a tight, self-sufficient pack of three. I have some canine friends like Dash, a Jack Russell, with whom I sometimes go salmon fishing, and Charmed-life Charlie, but they are not like the pack. I care very much what the rest of the pack thinks about me at any given time but I care as much about doglic opinion as the Chap does about the public variety.

In every pack there is supposed to be a 'peck-order' with under-members submitting to those above. None of us in our pack has a beak, however – though, on second thoughts, perhaps the Chap has. If it was a bite-order I would have a decided advantage. The bigger the pack the more the squabbles over peck-order but, happily, our pack is small so we don't have many arguments on that score. Being an only dog I am certainly not dog-pecked, as I might be if there were two of us. The Chap firmly believes he is the pack-leader, and he probably is up to a point, though I am not sure that he really understands his true position. One of our shooting pals, Johnnie Johnson, who was a great wartime fighter ace, wrote a book called *Wing Leader*. Perhaps

I'll induce the Chap to write one called *Pack-Leader* just to see exactly how much he is deluded. For instance, though he reckons that he decides when to take me out he usually does so because I have rousted him out of the study. I know exactly how to make him feel guilty of neglecting me by giving him a reproachful look. (He says I'm the Joker in the pack and he could be right.)

As I have related, my fame has had considerable effect on my status in the pack. But I agree with the Boss that it is best for all of us to let the Chap go on believing that he is the undisputed pack-leader and the Boss and I are just his right-hand bitches. It must be good advice because she has being doing it successfully for years. An honest dog will always bark the truth but, as all females know, there is a time when silence is more profitable and, besides, we must be kind and appreciative to dog's best friend and avoid pricking the balloon of his self-esteem. However, as the Chap well knows, in a wild-dog or wolf pack there is an element of democracy in that the leader can be deposed and, to some extent, remains in power by general consent. So he had better watch it! (I would like to change Church House to Pack House or The Den to remind me of my wolf ancestry, especially as the Chap gets fed up with being mistaken for the vicar by strangers who ignore the notice on the door – 'This is NOT the vicarage'.)

Startling evidence of the extent to which the Chap has accepted my position – and his wife's – are the green pullovers which they have been wearing round the village lately. On the front of his is my logo – my noble chocolate head on the front, complete with yellow collar, with DIDO in large chocolate letters. It is almost life-like enough for another dog to bark at it. The human heart is in the centre of the body, not on the left as commonly believed, so it gives me satisfaction to see him with my picture worn so near his heart for all to see. On his back are the words HER MAN – a walking admission of how possessed he is by me. His wife is similarly adorned but her back is labelled THE BOSS, a further public statement of my Chap's true position in our hierarchy. I say *my* Chap because I own him as much as he owns me and when I bark in his defence I am defending my property.

Considering that I am the other female in the Chap's life in a *ménage à trois*, the Boss treats us both surprisingly well. As we are both females in what is supposed to be a male-dominated world we stick together more than the Chap realizes.

The Boss is amazed every time she sees the Chap wearing his pullover because she thinks that he is the squarest man in the world when it comes to clothes. He still wears old suits with turn-ups and would rather die than be seen in jeans or trainers, yet he has been seen wandering in his Dido pullover on the river, at show-grounds and game fairs. In fact, the whole thing was his idea. He ordered the pullovers from a knitting company run by a shooting friend of ours in Stockbridge and we all went there to collect them, stopping, of course, at my favourite pub, The Mayfly, where the spiced ham is delicious and dogs are allowed at the outside tables. He chickened out, though, when it came to wearing his pullover at Cruft's, when I was in the Parade of Dog Personalities there, though the Boss didn't and wore hers for all to see. Still, I mustn't poke too much fun at the pack-leader, at least not in print, especially as we are so alike in so many ways, enjoying so many things together, even our silences. For example, like me, when he is bored he goes to sleep. We both have an exaggerated sense of the ridiculous. He has also reached the age when he is living by the day, as I have always done. As I have observed in another connection, if fate had intended otherwise, he could have made quite a good dog.

Naturally, we have our differences. For instance, the Chap talks about 'attacking' the day, when all I want to do is to embrace it. I am never moody, at least I don't think I am but I suppose that I could be deluded, seeing how often the Chap is. He certainly has his eccentricities. While some insomniacs count sheep leaping over a fence he counts salmon leaping up a waterfall. He resents foreigners, but who can accuse him of colour prejudice when he adores chocolate me and would still do so if I was jet-black? He spends a lot of time on the floor with me because he thinks that to understand us, humans should come down more to our level and see us as we really live. But his biggest eccentricity is his attitude to time. 'Man's enemy is the clock,' he says, 'woman's is the mirror.' He says he's like a pregnant woman – he finds it difficult to relax while he's in labour and he always is. It seems to me that he keeps going in order to keep going. I appreciate that when you are old you can't be patient because patience takes time and time is something you might run out of but, sometimes, I think that the Chap doesn't know whether he's turned the corner or gone round the bend. (No doubt I have my own eccentricities but they are irrelevant to this discussion.)

All in all though, the Chap is very much a 'hands-on' pack-leader and I like that, especially when the hands are stroking my ears or tickling my rump. The fondling is a form of affection and the canine–human bond needs the regular reinforcement of affection expressed as touching or verbal and gestural praise. I need to reciprocate and have my affection accepted as it would be in a pack.

Considering the disparity in our ages – seventy-three years – we get on famously. But then I suppose that he treats me like a grandchild to whom the elderly are always more indulgent than they were to their own children.

Fortunately, we share so many interests and my literary endeavours have forced him to spend even more time on me and with me. As he puts it, the tail now wags the man, though I prefer to think that he's my Chappie and I'm his pedigree chum. (My worst yet, I think.) Anyway, we are both very content with our mutual dependence, sharing the belief that those who do not experience the dog–man relationship miss one of the most rewarding joys life has to offer. The Chap says you are never alone with a dog and that there is nothing in life more welcome than the intruding snout of a well-loved bitch. He goes so far as to believe that a home without a dog is just a building. More and more people are realizing that and the full meaning of the relationship between humans and pets (not a word I like) is now the subject of serious study. Odd as he is, I must do everything to keep him going because I couldn't stand another traumatic change of pack, a pack-leader a bitch knows being better than one she doesn't know.

The best contribution I can make to that end is to lavish my affection on him. To achieve happiness and fulfilment both humans and dogs need to love and be loved. Both the human and canine species have an inherited loathing of loneliness, a fear really, because it was so dangerous, way back in time, for either of us to be on our own, separated from the pack. Alone, we could not defend ourselves against danger-ous predators or hunt down our prey successfully.

'Whosoever is delighted in solitude is either a wild beast or a god,' some philosopher said and I am neither. 'Solitude prompts us to all kinds of evil,' another one wrote, with lonely humans in mind, but when do we dogs get into trouble? When we are left alone and are bored and unhappy. As all this has become more widely appreciated more people are taking pity on only dogs, as I am, left on their own for hours when their families are out, by providing dog-sitters. I think it is a marvellous idea and, on the odd occasions when my couple have gone abroad, leaving me desolated, they have provided nice living-in ladies for the whole time they were away. I have my favourites but it is better not to name them as it may upset the others.

Kind as they were, they could not replace my real pack members. Not only was I deprived of my morning ritual but of the night rites, when the Chap beds me down on my beanbag and we have a game with the last treat of the day which he conceals in his hand and challenges me to extract without nipping him. I consoled myself by finding odd items belonging to the Chap or his wife and having them bed with me.

Those tender occasions when the Chap caresses me are not one-sided. Apart from the pleasure which he gets from displaying his affection it now seems that he acquires medical advantages. Research has shown that the act of stroking a dog lowers human blood pressure. The most recent studies show that having a dog companion reduces the chance that its owners will get heart disease, probably by reducing the level of dangerous cholesterol and fat in the blood, through exercise. Dogs are now being taken into hospitals and old people's homes to exert their benign influence. Some doctors are said to be prescribing dogs but you can't get one on the Health Service – yet. Though some do-gooders may well complain that the dogless are being 'deprived' by Government stringency.

Naturally, I am trying to get it into the Chap's head that the more time he spends stroking and fiddling around with me the longer he is likely to live, for I am prepared to sacrifice my time in such a noble cause. The whole thing is a real bonanza find for dogs and the explanation may lie in your ape ancestry. If you watch a pack of chimps, gorillas or baboons they are always grooming each other and this helps to calm them down and to relax. You can't be seen doing this – at least, not in public – but you can stroke your dog. Perhaps that fills a void in your modern culture.

I also suspect that there is a deep-seated need in the make-up of most humans for a close relationship with some other species, such as a dog or a cat, which harks back to the nobler days before man regarded himself as the God-appointed overlord of creation with absolute dominion over the 'brutes'. Primitive peoples looked on themselves as interlocked with all the creatures around them in the tapestry of nature. They treated them with respect and almost apologized when forced to kill them for food or clothing.

In view of all that, it is astonishing to us that so many of you are prepared to break up an established pack by separation and divorce, with appalling consequences for the canine members who may end up suddenly unwanted, in rescue centres or worse, with inevitable psychological trauma. Such cases often lead to tug-of-dog situations with couples squabbling over custody. In America there are lawyers specializing in such cases as well as in defence of dogs accused of excessive barking and other crimes. With business booming, they list themselves under 'Dog' in the Yellow Pages of the telephone directories.

The problem is complicated by the fact that, in human law, dogs are deemed to be property, like farm animals, and judges treat them like chattels. Some of their owners have a quite different attitude, however, and, even before telling their partners that they want a divorce, consult an expert in canine law to find out how they can be sure of keeping the dog or, at least, ensure visitation rights or a share of custody. The outcome of the bitter arguments may depend on whether the judge is a dog lover or a dogophobe. It often leads to an award of canimony, as well as alimony, to ensure that a single-family dog lives in the style to which it was accustomed.

I am confident that I am immune to any such danger because I put my faith in the widely advertised principle that those who worship together stay together – especially when the object of their veneration is a dog.

I am told that Mark Twain said, 'The more I see of my fellow men the more I love my dog.' Bark Twain would have put it, 'The more I see of my fellow dogs the more I love my Chap – and, of course, the Boss.'

No dog is an island entire unto itself – but a dog, a man and a woman can be.

14 The Birds and the Bees

*One is nearer dog's heart in a garden
Than anywhere else on earth*

I am extremely fortunate in having it understood by the rest of the pack that the whole of our garden, like the rest of the house, is part of my territory, to which I am usually entitled to have access at all times of the day or night. In that respect I suppose I could be called a dog of property. Completely walled-in gardens have special charm for gardeners, providing privacy and protection as well as vertical surfaces for growing plants, but they are even more welcome for dogs. I never need to be tethered when in the garden, to which I have immediate access through two dogs flaps. Nobody and no dog can get in or see in, so I can be completely relaxed when I am attending to a bone on the lawn. Once, when I was out in the car with the Boss, the Chap put my food out so that it would be waiting for me on my return, as I naturally expect. As the back gates had been left open the dog that lived next door came in and ate it. That grave error has never been repeated.

I can also use the lawn, without fear of interference, for just lying on my back with my legs in the air or what the Boss calls 'contemplating my navel' – though why I shouldn't do that with gratitude I don't know. After all, it sustained me during the long dark days of my gestation.

The road area immediately outside the back doors also counts as my territory, which is clearly stated on a notice with my picture on it in glorious chocolate-colour – *Do not enter – Dog running free*. I was incensed when the notice was removed from its frame and stolen by louts with which this village abounds. They were lucky that I could not get at them! Anyway, a new notice is back now.

There is a three-inch gap at the bottom of the back doors and through it I can spot people and dogs passing. If I am out there alone I wait quietly and then let them have a loud bark. It's fun to watch them jump and the dogs and I can then have a shouting match which usually brings the Chap running out, by which time I am back sitting peacefully on the lawn looking as though nothing has been happening.

I enjoy helping the Chap, who is something of a reluctant gardener because he would always rather be on the river, by staying out with him, giving him moral support and, occasionally livening him up when he is bending down by pushing a log I have taken off the pile into his posterior.

I do quite a bit of digging myself, though never when he is watching, and according to my book, am being helpful by root-pruning his roses, though that is never the way he sees it. I am resigned to the fact that my gardening endeavours will always be misunderstood. The big holes which I dug when I was pregnant (and also when I just thought I was pregnant) created a minor mystery which the Chap has never resolved but led him to enunciate Newton's Fourth Law – if all the earth is collected up after a dog digs a hole it will never refill it. In fact, there will always be a sizeable gap for which more earth will be required. Where did it go? I certainly hadn't eaten it and he couldn't find it. Anyway, he has become resigned to accepting that digging holes is an essential part of the canine culture and that I am justified in regarding part of the garden as my recreational sandpit. Frankly, when I see what trouble some other dogs cause to their owners, I realize how lucky mine are, though I would not have the bad taste to mention it.

Because the lawn is always handy and I have my dog flaps I don't necessarily have to be taken out to do you know what, as most dogs do. As with all things there is a drawback, though. Leaving it for Nature to call means that I have to venture out in all weathers. The Chap says there is something of the camel in all females but eventually I have to go and brave any storm which might be raging. Humans wouldn't like it. They'd say they were 'deprived' if they had to go to an outside loo where, at least, there is shelter once they get there.

The Chap has devised a special implement for picking up my manurial deposits, and then chucks them on the back of the borders, arguing that all that nitrogen which comes in my tins of food needs to be conserved. I have noticed that his aim has improved with practice but, occasionally, one goes astray and needs a second shot.

I am indebted to my friend, Willy Poole, that witty Northumbrian farmer and country sportsman who writes in the *Sunday Telegraph*, for a more immediate use for my deposits. They could be mixed with water and made into a paste and applied with a brush to deter rabbits and deer from nibbling the garden plants. Called Canina, this concoction is supposed to have been invented by the Spanish to keep sheep and goats from nibbling their vines. There is a use for everything but, fortunately, our walled garden is free from such intruders because I fear that the Chap would not be able to resist trying it, being very organic. He could not get much more organic, could he?

I am sure he would use Canina, irrespective of the smell, if it was effective against some other intruders – the crows and jackdaws which raid the song-birds' nests and devour the young ones. It would then save me a boring job – being a scarecrow on behalf of blackbirds, though we have so many in our garden that we might have enough to bake in the nursery-rhyme pie. This followed an episode when a pair of very tame blackbirds had built a nest just outside the conservatory door. It was their third brood that year and they had just reared four youngsters almost to the point where they were fully feathered. The Chap had found that the hen bird was so tame that he could feed her with soft bread while she sat on the nest, and was astonished by how often she missed it. Sometimes she knocked the bread out of his hands which pleased me because I was usually standing underneath and nabbed it. He bawled me out but, surely, the dog can eat of the crumbs that fall from the rich man's bird's nest? Sadly, just before the baby birds were due to quit the nest, jackdaws took two of them early one morning. The mother bird had been so scared that she took off and for four days the father fed the remaining pair and kept them going, though he would not sit on them at night. Fortunately, it was very warm, otherwise they might have died of hypothermia. Every time a crow or jackdaw appeared on the bird table, in a tree or on the ground I was encouraged to leap out of the door. They saw that I meant business and it worked, except that sometimes I saw off the cock blackbird by mistake. They do look alike. Though, like all dogs, I have the misfortune to be colour blind, I can see black but they could hardly expect me to distinguish between size. A black bird is a black bird and that goes for a blackbird.

I'm not an early riser so to deal with the jackdaws, which are, the Boss set up an inanimate scarecrow made out of a stepladder and plastic bags and left it out all night. It worked and if only they had thought of it earlier the mother bird might not have deserted. Anyway, full marks to Cock Blackie for a great job, especially as his wife returned on the fifth day to the absolute astonishment of the Chap and the delight of the Boss. She helped to feed the two young, though she did not sit on them, and in two more days they were out of the nest and bobbing about the garden, with the Boss being even more intent on keeping the jackdaws away.

In addition to being a scarecrow I am also expected to be a scarecat and that, I have to say, comes naturally. I confess that I do not like cats and, because they are worse than crows at killing young song-birds, the Chap shares my antipathy. He does not like cats because they kill birds though he used to kill pheasants, partridges and grouse whenever he got the chance. One shout of 'Pussy!' and I am through the flap doors in a flash. They say that dead cats tell no tales but I have not managed to catch one yet. So far, they have always reached a tree, leaving me barking helplessly on the ground, which explains the term cat burglar and why there is no dog equivalent. If only I had a dogapult!

The Boss turned against cats too, especially during the emotional blackbird saga. When it was all over I wondered, as they had both been such fusspots about a couple of blackbirds, what they would be like with my pups. Well, now I know, of course. Besotted!

Collared doves, which have invaded my territory and make such a mournful noise that they would be more appropriate next door in the graveyard, are even cheekier than the sparrows, coming into the conservatory to peck at grain that used to be spilled by the canary. I reckon they are fair game if I can catch one. I used to enjoy rousting them out of the trees in the evening but I was not allowed to do that once they built a nest in the cherry tree. Sadly, crows or jackdaws took their young ones too.

The Chap and the Boss go to great lengths to provide nesting sites with lots of nest boxes and ivy and other plants growing up the walls. He even cut holes in the doors of the outhouses so that robins could get in and nest there, safe from the neighbours' cats. For the last two years swallows have nested there, flying straight through one of the holes at great speed though it is not much wider than their wing-span. I belt through my dog door when there is a cat to chase but I would never risk it at that speed! The Boss is pleased because it has kept the swallows out of the garage. One swallow may not make a summer but two swallows can make a hell of a mess on the Boss's car.

They are both so daft about birds that all the hair from my brushings and the clippings from the Chap's hair, when the Boss cuts it, go out into the garden to provide nesting material for robins, hedge sparrows, chaffinches and other birds. Then, at the end of the season when we remove the used nests to make sure that the favoured sites are available for next season, we examine them to see if we can find traces of what was once part of us. Usually we find them. The hedge sparrows, in particular, favour my hair, weaving it into the lining with moss, of which there is always plenty on our lawn. One of their nests was lined with a mixture of my hair and the Chap's – ah!

I tell you, there is nothing wasted in this establishment and I am only surprised that he has found no use for the old nests, such as making them into soup, for instance, like the Chinese do. Instead he destroys them because he says they all contain bird parasites.

Last year, our nest examination solved a mystery which had annoyed me because I had been falsely accused which, of course, is common enough in the life of any dog. The Boss, who uses all manner of herbs in cooking, had planted a couple of sprigs of rosemary in a pot and, one morning, they had disappeared. I was suspected of having pulled them out for fun and eventually we found them up the cherry tree in the nest of the collared doves. I duly received an apology and a biscuit as a sweetener.

Sadly, there are no rabbits, which I would love, and the only intruders, apart from cats, have been hedgehogs which can squeeze in through the gap under the garden doors. Both the Chap and the Boss believed that they had seen a baby hedgehog scurrying into the big border and thought that this might explain the missing rosemary sprigs. I could have brought the offender in. Instead I thought it more fun for them to let his existence remain a mystery and watch their antics. It paid off because the Chap got the idea of putting out a saucer of milk for it, while I wasn't looking, in a place where he thought I wouldn't wander. Sure enough, each morning he found that it had been lapped up, convincing them that, indeed, we did have a prickly visitor, but I am afraid that I was the hedgedog which had enjoyed it in the darkness.

Being something of a naturalist, the Chap won't use anything that kills insects in the garden – not even flies which are a pest in my book. He is especially anxious to avoid killing bumble-bees in which the garden is rich. He is forever looking at them to determine their species. I avoid them because, since my unfortunate encounter when a pup, never disagree with a bumble-bee, has been my motto. I do chase the butterflies but the Chap doesn't mind because, with their jerky flight, I never catch one.

The only time the Chap and I seriously disagree over the garden is about his habit of attending to it when the sun shines so that by the time he is ready to take me out it is raining. I do wish that he would get his priorities right. Still, I suppose I should be grateful that he takes me out in all weathers, even when it's raining dogs and cats (one should never put cats before dogs).

15 Rarin' to Go

Oh Master, mine, where are we roaming?

I am very much an outdoor bitch and there are two kinds of 'outings' these days – outings in the line of duty and what I suppose are usually called 'walks'. When the Chap and I are invited, jointly, to open fêtes and fairs we are usually happy to comply, so long as they are in the country. Anything in London or a big city brings dismay and, generally, a turn-down from both of us. Personally, though, I was diffident about helping to open the Catholic Christmas Fair at Hungerford because, not long before the invitation came, the Vatican had ruled that a dog has no soul and so cannot enter Paradise, which I think is grossly unfair considering the virtuous life I have led and the pleasure I have given to so many people. When the Chap reminded me that the present Pope appeared to be having second thoughts on the issue I agreed to go and, jointly, we opened it. Since then I have had third thoughts, for reasons which I will explain at some length in a later chapter.

I thoroughly enjoyed opening the annual fête at Chilton Foliat, the next village, along with a new extension to the school there, because there were lots of children. All the Chap got was a rose for his buttonhole but I was presented with a lovely basket of treats which lasted for weeks at the rate the Chap doles them out. The headline in the local paper read 'Author opens fête and classroom' and though my minder was also present I took it as meaning me.

When I opened the Kintbury Autumn Fair the posters simply said, 'To be opened by Dido'. It was suggested that, for strangers, there should be some explanation of who Dido was, but the organizers decided that everybody knew, which I found very reassuring. As the Chap had been required to cut the ribbon on my behalf when we opened the school extension we decided that, in future, we must devise a way which would enable me to accomplish the cutting unaided. Necessity being the dam of invention, various high-tech ideas were considered, involving pushing buttons with my nose and so on but we settled for a simpler, more dependable and altogether more acceptable solution. We threaded the ends of two bits of ribbon into each end of a cooked sausage so that, when the moment arrived, I simply ate the banger and the ribbon fell apart. We practised it at home with the ribbon tied to two chair legs and I succeeded first time. Later, I realized that I had been too clever. If I had failed first time I might have got two sausages, so I was penalized for getting it right. As I have said, there is little justice in the world. Anyway, on the day, it worked a treat to loud applause all round, a happy occasion which was recorded, pictorially, in the local paper. Grave thought had been given to the type of sausage we should use. A hot dog was rejected because I do not like hot food and it sounded cannibalistic. A frankfurter might have done but we felt that, for an English country fair, such an alien would be out of place, Common Market or not. An English country sausage, made by the village butcher, was demanded. The Chap also had a back-up sausage in case a stray dog got into the hall and ruined the act. I got that as well, later. So that shall be my tried-and-tested method for opening fairs in future, though I think that we should always have a practice run first.

Briefly, my financial advisers considered the possibility that we might patent the device, as Dido's Fair and Fête Opener, but expert witnesses decided that it would be too easy to replace the banger with a chocolate bar or a biscuit. So I reveal the secret for all dogdom to use with my compliments.

One place I always enjoy is the Inglewood Health Farm just a few minutes from the house on the edge of our village. The clients, who are not all fat, as I expected they would be, like to be entertained in the evening, if only to help them forget food for a while, so the Chap takes me along and we do a double act – Dido and the Chap. It sounds a bit like a knock-about turn and perhaps it is, as he tells them stories about me and my books. At the end I pawtograph copies for anyone who wants them and the guests always make a great fuss of me. As the Chap says, any captive audience is not to be sneezed at by any author, canine or human, these tough days.

One of the things the Chap usually includes in our speech is his explanation of why all dogs can swim without being taught. He points out that all we do when we get out of our depth in water is to go on walking just as we would on land. As we are four-legged and our bodies are horizontal we are naturally buoyant, while a person who is upright in the water tends to sink. It seems that, as in the human world, there are exceptions to every rule in our world for, at the end of one of his dogspiels, a man came up to have his copy of my book signed and assured us that he had a dog which could not swim. 'It is a rather fat Boxer,' he explained, 'and on the few occasions when we have put him in water he sank like a stone and had to be rescued.' As I intimated to the Chap, there's always something new to learn about dogs. Age cannot wither, nor custom stale, their infinite variety.

Sometimes the Boss says that I should go into the health farm myself whenever I get overweight because, at least, it would get me away from the Chap who cannot resist giving me bits on the sly. I am sure I would enjoy the massage but that would be all because they wouldn't let me use the swimming-pool, not that I would appreciate the chlorine. Further, the Chap would never come into a health farm with me – he hates the idea of massage.

Because of my expertise on human behaviour I was invited by Robert Kilroy-Silk to take part in his morning TV programme, *Kilroy*, to help discuss all manner of important questions about the pet–human relationship, such as whether pets are exploited by their owners – a joke in my case – and why so many people need constant contact with living creatures apart from their own species. They sent a chauffeured car to take me to Teddington and, of course, my minder had to be with me. There were far too many creatures on the programme to make any worthwhile argument possible and though it was interesting to meet pythons, lizards, llamas, stick insects, giant spiders and parrots at close quarters, I was soon bored by it all and showed it when the camera focused on me – except, of course, when the Chap was presenting my views. Fortunately, we were sandwiched between two other people the Chap and I had wanted to meet – Lady Lucinda Lambton, a fellow eccentric, and Roger Mugford, the animal psychologist who designed some of my toys. Kilroy was very nice but he forgot to ask me about my book which brassed me off as, frankly, I would rather have been out walking.

There are two kinds of walks as far as the Chap is concerned, though they are the same to me – pointless walks, which are when he has to take me just for exercise, and purposeful walks, when he is bird-watching, spotting wild flowers – he is something of a flower-twitcher – or thinking aloud on his pocket tape-recorder. My walks in the village are much more eventful since I became famous. Everyone, well almost everyone, smiles and gives me a pat if they are near. Sometimes people want to shake my famous paw. Of course, I have some special friends like Elsie, the verger, who is eighty, and Janet, a neighbour who is ninety-two. They are the first to tell me that my picture is in the local paper. Inevitably, the Chap provides the odd laugh as we progress to the post-box and then back to the house via the allotments. One of the reasons is his knobbly blackthorn thumbstick, which is called Tripos because it serves as his third leg. It is silver mounted, with a great clonking metal ferrule at the bottom and we never go without it. When I am on heat he can use it to repel boarders but he reckons that even in country lanes, these days, and especially on tow-paths, it is not wise for us to be without a defensive weapon and I sense that he is dying for an excuse to wield it. We have sometimes lost it – left it outside shops and even on the Common – but everyone in the area knows Tripos so it always comes home.

The most rollicking in my dogalogue of recollections was the occasion when he measured his length on the pavement having slipped on a dog turd. For a few minutes his view about dogs in general was radically changed, especially as several people had witnessed the dog-doter's downfall and the cause of it. I had done my best to warn him by walking round it but, as usual, his thoughts were far away like those of the ancient philosopher who, with his eyes on the stars, fell down a hole in the ground. Sometimes he really is quite a pawful.

As I have mentioned, on another occasion when we were walking through the allotments expecting to see nothing special I caused a sensation by putting up a big roebuck which had been lying among the cabbages. It set off down a path and disappeared. The Chap couldn't believe his eyes and I doubt that anyone in the village believed him until somebody else saw the deer in his garden. It just shows what can go on in the dark or very early morning when nobody's looking.

The Chap always walks with me on the inside of the footpath, as a lady should be. I have heard that this used to be done so that the man's sword arm would be free to protect his female companion. Instead of a sword the Chap has Tripos, which I am sure he would wield in my defence, but his main purpose is to keep me from the traffic. This becomes more difficult every day with so many cars, vans and sometimes tractors, that the Chap calls the centre of our village 'Piccadilly Circus'.

I am repeatedly reminded of our very different environment, a foot or so off the ground, from yours, when the Chap tries to drag me behind a car in which the engine is running. At your height you have no idea what the exhaust fumes of a car are really like when they hit you full in the nose. I hate this gas attack so much that I just refuse to go behind a car when I spot that horrid stuff coming out of that dirty pipe. He always apologizes and takes me round the front. I promise you that, if you lived down at our level, the hue and cry against vehicle air pollution would be a lot louder than it is. Everyone knows that the carbon monoxide is very poisonous but so is the carbon dioxide. The Chap tells a story about a man who walked into a cave deep in a limestone mountain with his dog. He was all right but the dog died because there was a layer of heavy carbon dioxide on the ground. Then there is all the lead in that petrol. I wonder how many dogs have died of lead poisoning and may still be dying.

With the churchyard so near I am often being taken in and out of it, sometimes for appearances on TV, and, more than once, I have been a bride's first glimpse of an animal after being tied in wedlock. I am sure that the sight of a chocolate dog is preferable to that of a black cat, and luckier.

The great day in Kintbury which comes to us, rather than vice versa, and which I always enjoy is the May Day Fair (which they will call Fayre) usually held at the end of May. Our house is right in the middle of it and from 6 a.m. we cannot get the car out. Various bands and Morris dancers entertain the crowds in front of our windows and there are all sorts of stalls where the Boss, the Chap, or both, usually find a treat or two for me. Then, when it has all been cleared away by early evening, the Chap and the Boss can be guaranteed to take me down to the river because they are so keen to get out of the house for a spell themselves.

I described my walks on the Hungerford Common in my last book and since then there have been more adventures. One was a mystery which still remains unresolved. One November morning the Chap called me several times and when I took no notice he strode over in some dudgeon, as they say, to see what was interesting me. He was as astonished as I was. He found me staring at a large fish, a grayling of at least one-pound weight. It had no marks on it but the Chap decided that it must have been taken there by a heron which had caught it in the river about a quarter of a mile away, perhaps earlier that morning. Presumably the heron had taken the grayling there to eat it and had then been disturbed, though I can't see why it could not have swallowed it immediately after catching it, which is what they usually seem to do. He would not let me eat it though I am usually allowed to nibble a fresh grayling he has caught.

The Chap has pursued human moles all his professional life and the house is festooned with moles – wooden sculptures, etchings and even paperweights sent as presents to mark his mole-hunting activities. I prefer the moley ones – the ones in the velvet jackets – and pursue them on the Common whenever I can. The farmers regard them as pests and I thought we were in for a real adventure last May when those real pests, the hippies, were due to take over part of the Common, allegedly to celebrate some pagan feast, which they had done the previous year in spite of efforts by the police to stop them because they do so much damage. Instead, the police set great tree trunks across all the roads and, while they kept local cars out as well, they completely foiled the hippies who tried to move them but couldn't. It was just as well because, eventually, ten thousand of them turned up in the disused quarry where they finally held their festival. What a mess they would have made! And how many fleas would their dogs have left in the grass, apart from the human variety? The Chap says the worst parasites are the hippies themselves because they live on tax-payers' hand-outs, pay nothing back, have no intention of ever doing any work and, by their filthy appearance, deliberately make themselves unemployable.

Though the fishermen don't like it, I find the walks along the canal tow-path even more interesting since the canal was fully opened and lots of gaudily painted narrow boats, bedecked with flower pots, have begun to use it. Many of the moored narrow boats have dogs, with whom I usually make friends, and most of their owners have never seen a chocolate Labrador before. Further, boat people don't mind if I jump in for a dip like the fishermen do, though I make far less disturbance than a passing boat. A girl has to do something to get rid of the flies on a hot day. There are no flies on Dido – at least, not for long.

These boats have extraordinary names like *Ned Kelly*, with paintings of the Australian outlaw, or *The Merchant of Little Venice*, which comes from Regent's Canal in London. The Chap's favourite is *Mid-life Crisis*. He says he did lots of crazy things then, though nothing as rash as buying a boat.

The Kintbury entrance to the tow-path has recently been 'landscaped' by the canal authority at huge expense. I was surprised, and slightly miffed, that they did not get me to open it. Scores of trees and shrubs have been planted, creating a paradise for male dogs, and have been surrounded with tons of bark chips (I wonder why they call it bark) to keep the weeds down. What a hope! The weeds are through already in profusion but, meanwhile, it is great stuff for practising my shuffle after I have patronized it. You should see it fly!

Part of the landscaping is a car-park for the tow-path fishermen. They do their best to stay friends with the boat people but there will always be a conflict of interests. It is the same with the Chap and canoeists when they come down the Tay when we are salmon fishing. He waves at them but I can hear him cursing them under his breath. It is true enough that the canal was built for boats, but the fishermen preferred it when the locks had fallen into disuse and there was no through traffic. I like it when the Chap stops to gossip with the anglers. He is helping the Boss to collect true fishing stories for another book she is writing and it always cheers her up when we return with one or two new ones. So much so that I get an extra treat for my part in the effort. You see, he often uses my intrusion into some angler's reverie as an excuse for talking to him.

I think that the locks are the most interesting part of a canal and I used to enjoy looking over the edge as a lock filled up. But since there was an awful tragedy with children falling into a lock not far from here he won't let me near one any more. A pity! I like living dangerously. As I say, 'You have to risk it to get the biscuit.'

The Chap tends to be tough about people but is soft about ducks on the canal. Imagine his horror when I jumped at a duck which got up suddenly out of the reeds, and nearly caught it, when it had a flotilla of seven young with it. I don't know what humans mean when they say 'out for a duck' but I know what I mean and he saw it as eight potential tragedies. There are tragedies enough in duckdom because the mothers hatch out up to a dozen babies and as the days go by they disappear until the mothers end up with two or three and sometimes none at all. The Chap always blamed the ducks for being such poor mothers compared with the coots, which never seem to lose a youngster and are prepared to see me off if I go near one. Then, one day, we saw a sparrow-hawk swoop down and take a duckling. Another day we saw a jackdaw do the same thing. So, with the big pike taking a few as well, perhaps the mother ducks do not have much chance anyway. It's tough being a duck round here, especially when the shooting season opens.

Until then, though, the ducks do rather well, being fed lots of bread by locals and by visitors. As a result, they all fly with a great noise when anyone appears with a bag and, if the Chap happens to be recording some imperishable thought on his pocket tape-machine as we progress along the canal bank – as is his eccentric wont – there is a background of quacking ducks when he plays it back in his study.

The Chap takes me bird-watching and gets excited when he sees something unusual. There is a little lake close by the Avenue – a leafy lane where I can run free – and he was amazed to see about a dozen cormorants sitting around there. Presumably they were attracted by the coarse fish in the lake but maybe they raid the local trout farm at first light like the herons do.

He likes looking at little ponds even more than lakes and early last year I spotted something he had not seen since he was a boy – a ball of frogs. There, in shallow water, was, literally, a living ball made up of frogs all clinging to each other, mostly by the legs, hoping to spawn. Actually it wasn't all living for when the Chap separated the frogs there, in the middle, as he predicted there would be, was the corpse of one poor female. One male had grasped her and then a dozen others or more had tried to do the same thing suffocating the object of their lust. (I can hardly call it affection.)

For frog read dog! What a fate!

16 On Tour

There is a tide in the affairs of bitch,
Which, taken at the flood, leads on to God knows where

A change is as good as a romp, so I am all in favour of going away on visits to other parts of the country. As a much-travelled dog I would love to go abroad too if it were not for the quarantine restrictions. Beyond question, the highlight visit of 1992 was my appearance on the evening of 9 January in the Parade of Dog Personalities at Cruft's which, for bitches anyway, is the canine equivalent of the Miss World competition. Not being a show dog – for which I am eternally grateful – I never thought I would be a star at Cruft's Dog Show but there I was, invited by the Chairman of the Kennel Club for my literary achievement. I was wildly excited when the invitation came and our local paper, the *Newbury Weekly News* headlined the news, 'Literary dog to be honoured by Cruft's'. I certainly felt honoured and from that moment have regarded myself as a genuine VID. What had been just a bone-dream had become a reality.

We spent a couple of hours touring the show, held in the Birmingham Exhibition Centre, and visiting various stands, where I was sometimes recognized and always well received and where the Chap obviously fancied himself, rubbing shoulders with the *dognoscenti*. All manner of dog treats were available on the stalls, some free, others for sale, and the Boss went round making a selection for me. Inevitably, they lost each other in the crowded hall and the Chap got quite irritated, though it was his fault as much as hers. He was also fazed when he needed to go to the loo and found that dogs were not allowed in. He realized the danger that if he just left me tied up I might well be dog-napped or switched for some less attractive animal. Eventually, he induced some stranger, who had his wife and children with him, to hold me while he disappeared. I thought he was taking a chance and so must he because he was back in record time for an old man.

During our tour of the Show I had never seen or heard so many dogs all at once. I could hardly hear myself bark. They were all so different but, of course, I recognized them all as dogs, however small or peculiar. They were all very friendly, especially Chester from Staffordshire, a chocolate, who was judged the best Labrador puppy. He is one of the few chocolates to have won because, as several exhibitors assured us, some judges tend to be prejudiced against our colour. Imagine the outcry from certain quarters if that was to happen, so openly, in the human world!

In the evening the Personalities all met in the Collecting Ring and then moved into the Main ring in front of a huge crowd being later shown on TV. Of course, the Chap and I were not there to show but to show off and we did. I felt like a model on the dog-walk. He was interviewed about me on the radio, I was interviewed for TV by Angela Rippon and thought she was very nice even though she did accuse me, in front of millions, of revealing family secrets in my book. I suppose she is right really. I did, didn't I? Anyway, the Chap has forgiven me.

Surprisingly, I wasn't the only chocolate Labrador in the Parade. There was also Archie, who is a PAT (Pets as Therapy) dog. He had been bred for the gun but was so gentle that he was gun-shy so, instead, he visits schools to show the children how to interpret dog body-language. This helps them to know if a dog they happen to meet is safe to approach, not that any Labrador is likely to bite anyone. Personally, I can never stress enough that, in this day and age, people, and especially children, are in far greater danger from other humans than from dogs.

Archie's main job, though, is cheering up people who are in hospital, especially those who love dogs but cannot have one there. Contact with him reduces the impact of depression, loneliness and boredom. This is especially valuable in psychiatric hospitals, where so many patients are withdrawn, and an affectionate and understanding dog can help to pull them out of themselves. Psychiatrists are also using dogs like Archie to help to treat people who have a phobia about dogs, especially since all that publicity about 'killer' breeds. Some of them are so scared of dogs that they dare not go out for fear of being bitten and won't let their children out or go on holiday in case they meet strange dogs. A few encounters with Archie calm their fears. One of the Queen's former Corgis does the same thing and there are hundreds of other dogs giving this service now – all unpaid volunteers. Perhaps I will do it if ever I get any spare time. Funny to think of somebody's life being in my paws!

All PAT dogs must pass a temperament test to show that they are friendly and reliable, but I should not have any difficulties, especially as I am used to visiting one hospital already – the Hampshire Clinic near Basingstoke. The Boss underwent a major operation there in 1991 and she was greatly cheered when she saw me from the window. I cheered myself up at night while she was away by choosing her Barbour jacket from three which were hanging on chairs in the kitchen and also took her key-ring off the table, putting them on my beanbag and laying on them all night. I always go with her and the Chap when she goes back for medical check-ups. I have quite a few fans there and, while the Boss is inside, the Chap takes me around the waste ground behind where there are lots of rabbits. We are both immensely relieved when the Boss emerges, smiling, with a thumbs-up sign.

We now know that we could have lost the Boss but for the outstanding skill of a surgeon, and where would the pack have been then? Sometimes he comes to our place for dinner with his wife, who is called Bounce, which happens to be the name of a dog food I like. It's a small world, isn't it?

On the way back home from Cruft's, the Chap and the Boss put their minds to thinking up a suitable word for a muster of dogs, such as we had just seen. There is a pride of lions, a troop of baboons, a charm of goldfinches, a murmuration of starlings but nothing comparable for dogs because pack means something else, as I have explained. They settled for a constellation of canines because each of them is a star to someone.

As they burbled on I was thinking, seriously, about the possibility of setting up a human Cruft's, called Dido's, because, like Mr Cruft, I thought of it. Both men and women would take part and, ideally, should be judged by dogs who could bark the marks awarded. They would be graded not only on beauty but on poise, vigour and general behaviour. Not only is handsome is as handsome does but so is ugly. They would be required to trip round the ring, being on leads held by their dogs. I must give it more thought but, on one thing the Chap and I are already firm – show-biz people would be barred from the Parade of Human Personalities. We are all sick of them in our house.

A few days after our return the *Newbury Weekly News* did a feature about all the local dogs who had been shown at Cruft's but the part about me was on the top, which I don't think could have pleased the show people much.

Another highlight of our recent visits was to the nutrition research centre financed by Pedigree Pet Foods at Waltham on the Wolds, near Melton Mowbray, where those scrumptious meat pies come from, though I am sure that is a coincidence. The area is also famous for fox-hunting of which, I suppose, I should disapprove though, no doubt, I would get pleasure out of running with the hounds if I could. Like Mr Jorrocks, I love the fox but I love the hound more. As we turned into the road signposted to the Centre there was a dead fox which had obviously been killed by a car. Poor thing! At least the hunt gives it a fair chance.

When we arrived in the rather splendid reception area there was a notice up saying 'Welcome to Chapman Pincher and Dido'. What about that for fame! We were warned that there were two office cats which could be anywhere in the huge open complex but, though I looked everywhere in anticipation of an encounter, they never showed. A pity because I could have made a more memorable impact on the staff.

Dr Jo Wills, who is a vet but does not smell like one because she is engaged solely on food research, took us round. I had never seen or heard so many dogs in one place, though Cruft's, which came later, had more. A lot of them were Labradors but not one of them was chocolate. I met the old retired stud Labrador who had done it all and also his replacement who had it all to do and was obviously raring to go. The difference between quiet satisfaction and eager anticipation was self-evident. No unpleasant experiments are carried out at Waltham. All the dogs had palatial quarters and were well loved, but I was glad not to be one of them.

Pedigree Petfoods is owned by Mars, who make the bars I like so much, and, though I did not get any chocolate, there was a spin off from the lunch for me. Mars also make ice-cream bars which were served at the lunch. The Chap secured a mini-bar for me and, as it was a hot day, it went down a treat.

We then went to a factory to see how pet food is actually made. There were millions of tins rolling along conveyors in and out of enormous cookers – Chum, Lassie and Chappie. There was also Whiskas for cats, which is a waste of good meat, in my view. The Chap was more interested in the labelling machine and couldn't fathom how the labels could be whipped round the tin so accurately at such speed.

The machinery has to run seven days a week throughout the year, except for five days when everything stops for maintenance, showing how many cats and dogs there are. As the Chap remarked, we are in the wrong business. I came away ladened with dog treats and a big sack of a new dried food.

On the way home the Chap invented a new game. I was in the back of the estate car behind the dog-guard and the Chap started throwing treats through the bars – a most pleasant surprise. I am usually on the back seat but I don't mind being 'in the boot' so long as that game continues.

We stopped in the nice old town of Oakham and while the Boss went shopping the Chap took me for a stroll. We found the ancient stocks which used to be used to confine criminals in the open so that people could jeer and throw things like rotten eggs at them. What a pity they don't use them now for people who are cruel to dogs!

A few weeks later we returned to Melton Mowbray to visit the Defence Animal Centre, run by the Royal Army Veterinary Corps, at the invitation of the Commandant, Lieutenant Colonel Peter Roffey. That is where they train those brave dogs which protect defence establishments and sniff out hidden guns and explosives, and I was anxious to see how it was done. At the barrier we were challenged by soldiers toting machine-guns. It is hard to imagine why anyone would want to attack a dog-handling centre but the IRA was looking for soft targets and, apart from the chance to kill British soldiers, the terrorists also regard the dogs as enemies for reasons which soon became apparent.

We saw one black Labrador, oddly called Blue, being put through its paces after recovering from injuries inflicted by a cowardly attack by the IRA – a bomb thrown over the wall of the kennels – in Northern Ireland. It had been almost blown to dogdom come, suffering severe ligament damage but had made a good recovery. Sadly, its handler had been killed in the blast so it was being transferred to a new one whom we watched at work. A war hero, Blue was as keen as ever and had no trouble in finding a metal tube containing Semtex explosive. I was glad to hear, later, that he has now returned to 'arms and explosives search duties' but he will not be sent back to

Northern Ireland, where he has done more than his stint.

After the Chap's failure to teach me to retrieve a soft pheasant, he was lost in wonder to see a Springer Spaniel retrieve a hard, metal pistol, which had been cleverly hidden, and bring it back to his handler. He was trained to show when he had found it by the wag of his tail and general behaviour and to desist from picking it up until the handler joined him and ordered him to do so – a precaution in case the weapon was booby-trapped. After this performance I pretended not to hear the Chap's rather sarcastic comments about me.

Most of the three hundred dogs were German Shepherds, what the Chap prefers to call Alsatians, helped out by some Labradors, a few Springers and Rottweilers. Two huge constellations of canines in the Melton Mowbray area! That must give it particular distinction. Melton used to be associated with horses – again nothing to do with those pies, I am assured.

The dogs all come from the general community, usually when people need to dispose of their pets for various reasons and, while we were there, a security firm which was going into liquidation rang up offering four dogs which were already partly trained. Breeding is regarded as being of no importance. Courage is what counts and homes are found for any that are judged as lacking it after the first week.

The place is a canine monastery for no bitches are recruited there. The soldiers are better placed because quite a few of them are women. They are all volunteers who want to work with dogs so they are motivated in the right direction even before they reach the Centre. The closeness of the relationship which builds up between a dog and his handler reminded me of the closeness between me and my Chap. Each soldier is encouraged to sit in his dog's enclosure and we saw one stretched out while tickling the belly of a black Labrador lying upside down, just as I do. It was regarded as an essential part of the soldier's daily work!

I must say that the Army has gone out of its way to give the dogs the best possible environment. Each has a custom-built, draught-proof wooden kennel and lots of posts have been put up in the exercise field, which is treeless, so that they are available to be patronized. Nobody bothers about poop-scoopers and we were all warned to tread warily in what must be one of the most regularly manured grass fields in Leicestershire.

Apart from being a bitch, I would be no good because the dogs are trained to be aggressive against anyone whom the handler suspects, and I might find that difficult. We watched a line of Alsatians being trained to be aggressive by soldiers acting as baiters. They were all well-padded and needed to be because the dogs sometimes got hold of them. The dogs are highly intelligent and know that they are not to attack anyone until the handler orders them to do so. When on duty or being trained they wear a harness and as soon as that is put on they know that play has ended and work has started.

There is only one sadness about their lives. When patrolling the perimeter fence of a defence establishment they may walk as much as fourteen miles every day, so they tend to be old by the time they are eight or nine when, I trust, I shall be still in my prime. On reaching the end of their working days they can never be returned to civilian life because of their aggressiveness. The handlers are not even allowed to have their dogs at home because of the risk of attacking a wife or child. So they have to be put to sleep. Like old soldiers, they fade away. I wonder if they are buried with military honours. They deserve to be.

Later that day we went on to the RAF at Wittering, just off the Great North Road, where the Chap was talking to an RAF conference about spies and intelligence. There was even greater security there, with a machine-gun pointing at us out of a pillbox and, of course, guard dogs. The security was so tight that, as we were all staying the night, the Chap and the Boss had to learn a code to open the doors. Everyone made a fuss of me and paid me compliments which are always welcome to the female ear, but the best part was the rabbits on the lawn. I had to sleep in the car but the Chap found the RAF beds so hard that he said I was better off there.

We did not have to stay the night when we visited the training centre for Guide Dogs for the Blind because it was near by – at Wokingham in Berkshire and, even more aptly, in Barkham Road! We had been invited by Ray Smith, the Controller, who had read my book, and when the Chap, the Boss and I entered the big establishment we were struck by the tremendous sense of care which pervaded it, both for the dogs and the blind people being trained to use them. There are cosy bedrooms, where the blind 'students' stay for the three-week course, canteens, splendid kennels for the dogs, usually in pairs for company, and a veterinary hospital. No wonder the Guide Dogs Association needs so much money! With a young blind person it may be committed for fifty years, paying for all the dog food, vets' fees and maintaining contact with visits and letters in Braille.

The sheer size of the enterprise was astonishing as Mr Smith and Dick Michael, the training manager, showed us round. Though this was just the training centre for the south-east there is a staff of ninety and a regular population of about one hundred dogs. The Association has its own breeding station, near Leamington, producing up to one thousand pups a year for the seven main training centres – mostly yellow Labradors, which are more visible than a white stick, Golden Retrievers and crosses between them. When six weeks old they are farmed out to people who look after them until they are about a year old when they 'go to school' at a training centre. The course lasts about nine months and we saw dogs being trained to take people up and down steps, cross busy roads and avoid obstacles. I was lost in wonder and felt proud to be a dog. About 80 per cent, both dogs and bitches, qualify and the rest go to homes as pets. Sadly, though understandably, they have to be sterilized because sex and its various canine consequences would be too intrusive and distracting. Remember that whenever you see a guide dog. It has made a big sacrifice to help a human being.

Each blind student and guide dog have to be matched to be happy with each other because the relationship becomes so inter-dependent. The worst problem arises when a guide dog nears retirement – at about ten – and needs replacement or if it dies. In either case, the blind owner grieves so much that the Association pays great attention to bereavement counselling.

We were very touched by a story told by Dick Michael, who had previously been a regular soldier. During a riot in Northern Ireland he had been struck on the head with a brick, suffering such injury that he had to be invalided out of the Army. He felt that fate had been extremely unkind until, a few months later, his friend, with whom he could well have been on duty, was blinded by a bomb. The friend eventually came to be trained and equipped with a guide dog. As Dick, said to us, 'It's a funny old world!'

While everyone knows the stupendous work which dogs do for the blind, few are aware of the remarkable effort made by dogs in serving as ears for the deaf. I did not really appreciate it myself until I saw a demonstration in the ring at Cruft's when I was there in 1991. So, later, we all visited the training centre for these Hearing Dogs for the Deaf at Lewknor, a village on the eastern edge of Oxfordshire. I was welcomed by Gillian Lacey, one of the founders, and her dog, Gemma, who is now a reception dog and was very friendly. They have about twenty dogs in training at any one time and place about forty-five with deaf people, at no charge, every year. They are mainly mutts, because they come from rescue centres, and are usually small or medium-sized.

We saw dogs being trained to run and warn their deaf owners when the doorbell rang, the telephone, the alarm clock, the cooking pinger, the baby alarm or the smoke alarm. When they are out walking they inform their owners if anyone is approaching from behind and, of course, warn about any intruders in the house. Some deaf owners learn to speak to their dogs in sign language, which is how dogs communicate with each other when we meet.

Apart from doing these marvellous services, the dogs give companionship and greatly reduce the sense of isolation and loneliness. In fact, some of the deaf people say that the dog makes their life much more worth living, which both the Chap and I can appreciate. Deaf people become more confident and independent once they become 'dog-eared'. They tend to go out more and, as with guide dogs, Marks & Spencer permit registered hearing dogs, which wear bright orange coats, to go into their stores. This does not surprise me as the M & S Life President, Lord Sieff, who is a close friend of mine, is one of the kindest men I know.

The training is all done by treats. Wendy, one of the trainers, got into bed in the training flat and, when her alarm clock went off, her little fluffy-haired pupil, Pebbles, raced upstairs and jumped on to her bed, getting a treat for her trouble. The clever little dog did the same when the doorbell rang and also alerted Wendy when she was in a different room and the telephone rang. What was the good of being told the telephone is ringing if the person being called is deaf? The answer was that many deaf people can hear a telephone conversation with a special electronic aid.

The whole training takes about four months so, in that time, each dog does jolly well for treats and, to reinforce their lessons, they need to be given treats occasionally by the deaf people they are looking after. So it's a good life being a 'hearing dog', especially when the alternative is being unwanted in a rescue centre. The training costs about £2,500 and many of the dogs are sponsored by kind individuals and organizations. Understandably, the dogs are in great demand and Hearing Dogs for the Deaf, a Charity, is hoping to open more training centres soon.

So far, the Chap has not gone deaf though I am surprised he hasn't considering the number of cartridges he has fired through his guns. I should be thankful, I suppose, that I did not do much shooting because the noise can make a gun dog deaf too, as happened to some of the Chap's Spaniels though, no doubt, being addicts, like him, they thought it had all been worth it. The visit made me appreciate how awful it would be to be deaf myself – unable to hear the buzz of the can-opener, unable to bark when the doorbell rings or another dog passes by. Unable to hear the screech of the Chap's reel when he hooks a big fish. Unable to hear my pups' squeaks. Unable to hear all the nice compliments the Chap, the Boss and other people pay me. Perhaps there should be Hearing Dogs for

Deaf Dogs as well as Hearing People for them. If I get time I will work on it.

Just as most women like going to fashion houses, I enjoyed going to visit the place that makes the yellow nylon Canac collars which are now my logo. The factory is housed in an old mill – Becks Mill in the Wiltshire town of Westbury, where they made gloves years ago. James Blair, who runs the place, was very kind, welcoming me and presenting me with the first collar to have a dog's name woven into it by new technology involving some magic machine. When I am wearing it, as I do on special occasions, people do not need to wonder if I am Dido. They can read that I am. Mr Blair also presented me with a matching yellow lead.

I have quite a collar wardrobe now, all Canacs, giving me the occasional change which all females like. As they become too discoloured to wash any more the Chap keeps topping them up so that I can't complain that I have nothing to wear, as the Boss does occasionally, though her wardrobes are packed with clothes. On the way back home we passed Silbery Hill and all climbed to the top. There's supposed to be some Iron-Age chief buried there, perhaps with his Iron Age dog.

When I went to the moors to chase grouse I was fitted up with an extra plastic collar impregnated with something that repels sheep ticks which also like dogs. Now scientists have come up with the ultrasonic flea collar which works by surrounding the wearer with an ultrasonic beam that reflects back off the ground. The fleas are not supposed to like it and jump off. It has a battery which can be replaced when it is run down but I wouldn't like to wear one until I can be sure what the waves do to me.

I can get hot enough under one collar without two, for dog's sake!

17 Over the Border

Nowhere beats the heart so kindly
As beneath the tartan plaid (or collar)

Being in Scotland is a dream the whole pack shares, and every time we go, which is usually twice a year, I am taken to new places as well as visiting houses which are like second homes to me. I love to see my Scottish friends, human and canine, and to make new ones. I am gradually learning the language which, of course, is fully understood by Scottish dogs, some of which cannot understand English. Say 'Down!' to a Scottish dog and it will probably do nothing. Say 'Doon!' and doon it gets. It's the same with 'Get oot', when a man wants his gun dog to retrieve a bird.

The Chap, in particular, would love to have some Scottish blood – I suspect that he might then wear a kilt – and kids himself that, because some of his female ancestors lived not far from the border, some hairy-kneed Scots raider might have had his way with one of them. (I didn't really know what that meant but, since my trysts with Bugler, I do now.)

Sometimes, on the way, we stay overnight in Northumberland at a house called Fallodon, which once belonged to a famous fisherman and bird-watcher called Earl Grey, who is also immortalized in a kind of tea which the Chap hates. The house has lovely lawns and places for me to run, and the owners are real dog-lovers. After leaving there one morning I was taken to Flodden Field near the village of Branxton in Northumberland, just south of the border. The Chap and the Boss took me to the top of Piper's Hill, quite a climb for them but an easy run for me, where there is a memorial cross to more than 10,000 Scots and English who killed each other in hand-to-hand combat in only two hours on the afternoon of 9 September 1513. The 9,000 Scots who died included the flower of the nobility – King James IV, many earls, barons, knights and even bishops with, of course, their retainers. What lunacy! What a way to spend an afternoon! No conflicting packs of dogs, wolves or any other animals would ever inflict comparable suffering on each other. The memorial has a simple plaque – 'To the brave of both nations'. They were brave all right, but they were also foolish. I reckon that man's basic nature has not changed all that much in the four centuries which have elapsed – either with respect to his ferocity or stupidity.

We witnessed another tribute to man's intelligence and culture when the Chap took me into the empty little Branxton church to buy a pamphlet which told us that all the bodies had been collected there for burial. So it was a hallowed spot for Scots and English alike. When it came to paying the 50p the Chap could not see any collecting-box but eventually spotted a slit for the money at the top of a strong steel pipe let into the floor and connecting with a box in the crypt which was locked. That was the only way the parson had been able to stop the takings being stolen! And they say that Labradors are greedy!

Crossing the border is always a thrill for the Chap and the Boss though, except for a marking stone, the countryside looks no different. It also smells the same until we reach the heather and the pines but I share in their excitement, especially as it is the nearest I can get to going abroad. As Doggie Burns would have put it, 'O saw ye bonnie Dido, As she gaed o'er the border?' What might happen, though, if the Scots got home rule? Would we all be held up at border posts and customs? Would I be allowed in and out? What might happen if rabies was brought into the south of England by a fox running through the Channel Tunnel or hiding in a railway truck? Might I and my like be barred at the border? All our pack fervently hopes that we do not live to see the end of the Union.

I love it, especially, when we go through an area called the Sma' Glen, which looks like Scotland ought to look – 'Caledonia, stern and wild', knobbly hills and lots of heather, with a few places where I am allowed to run. We always stop in a little place called Amulree where there is a pub which serves teas with scones, jam and cream, of which I get my share. Sadly, in many parts of Scotland, huge areas of heather have been replaced by millions of coniferous trees which may offer limitless opportunity for male dogs but are of no interest to me. There is nothing to chase in those deep, dark plantations.

If we are going to fish the Dee we stay in a most comfortable hotel in Banchory where the owners are good friends of mine. Called Banchory Lodge, it has fishing of its own and I can watch the salmon jumping when I am sitting waiting in the car. The Dee is a lovely clean river for me to swim in because with the Monarch up the Glen – at Balmoral – nobody has dared to pollute it. At least not yet, but with the sad slump in respect for the royal family anything seems possible now.

One of our favourite beats at Banchory is called Inchmarlo and the gillie there told a cautionary tale for fishing dogs who are also gun dogs. Near the end of a long battle with a very large salmon, the angler was standing on a jetty just above some rapids. The gillie shouted, 'You'll have to bring it in now if you are going to get it.' Unfortunately, 'Get it' was the command which the angler used when he wanted his big Springer Spaniel, who was by his side, to retrieve a pheasant. In jumped the Springer, straight on to the salmon which swam off as the hook broke away. His master was furious but he was only obeying instructions. A dog's a dog for a' that.

I love it when the Chap decides to go out again to fish in the gloaming – the twilight which is much longer in Scotland. Sometimes, though not always, salmon which have stayed quietly asleep all day suddenly come alive when the sun goes down, jumping about and taking the fly which they ignored all day. The Chap gets wildly excited when this happens. So do I and I hope that the twilight of my years will be a gloaming.

Our most favourite Scottish base is Kinnaird Estate, near Dunkeld in lovely Perthshire, where we stay with my very special friend, Connie Ward, who, though she is an American by birth and female, is called the laird. There was great excitement as we arrived because a baby hedgehog had taken up residence in the garden, but I am afraid that I soon spoiled that. As soon as I tried to make friends it wanted to be off and quickly legged it up the hill at quite a remarkable pace for such a small creature. The rabbits are resident, however, and gave me a few close encounters of the furry kind.

Most of the time we fish the Tay there but, from Kinnaird, one can take off for the day to all sorts of wonderful places famous in history. One of the nearest is the narrow Pass of Killiecrankie, where there was a battle in 1689. The River Garry which runs through the pass is narrow there and we went down to see the Soldier's Leap where a soldier jumped across to save being captured or killed. Those chasing him didn't have the courage to try. The rocks were nasty but I am sure I could have done it with a run though I would have much preferred to swim across. Perhaps the soldier couldn't swim. It is odd that even the Scottish gillies who spend their working lives on water are rarely able to swim and sometimes pay the penalty for it.

It is also a nice run past various lochs where I was allowed out for a drink and a dip on the way to the Vale of Glencoe – the so-called Vale of Weeping, where the Macdonalds were massacred by the Campbells. There seem to be plenty of Macdonalds left and I suppose that, though the name is spelled slightly differently, the places that sell those juicy hamburgers were set up by one of them. So I have to approve of the Macdonalds, though I have an equal liking for Campbell's soups. I noticed an advertisement for Campbell's soups not far from the Vale. I am surprised that some Macdonald hasn't torn it down.

Most names seem to begin with Mac in Scotland, which I understand means 'son of'. We even met a chap called MacSporran and you can't get more Scottish than that, though the Chap insists that one of his soldiers in the war was called MacHaggis. He might, of course, be pulling my leg, which he sometimes does to get his revenge for the tricks I play on him though, on the whole, I think I have more success than he does. Anyway, I like the Macs, especially those Big Macs. Perhaps we should have called one of my male pups MacDido.

While Scotland is celebrated, worldwide, for haggis, which I like, it has also become famous for black-puddings which the Chap says are really associated with Yorkshire. One day, while we were lunching at the Kinnaird Hotel, one of the Scottish guests, who is a butcher, told us that he had just returned from Belgium where he had won the international cup for the world's best black-puddings. His greatest pleasure was in beating the Belgians who really fancy themselves as black-pudding makers. When presenting the cup, the Belgian official said how pleased he was that the cup had gone to England, which did not please the Scottish victor! He promised to send a sample to the hotel and I was looking forward to passing my judgement but, sadly, as so often happens with human promises made on the spur of the moment, it never arrived. (Perhaps this mention will jog his memory.)

When we went further north towards Inverness, where the Chap and the Boss were going to fish another river called the Spey, we stopped for lunch on the shore of Loch Rannoch and, as it was windy, I experienced my first big waves when I went for a swim. My immediate response was to try to stop them washing over my face by biting them but it had no effect. I am told that some old king with a name like Canute (which probably meant he had something to do with a dog) had a similar experience. Time and tide wait for neither man nor dog.

When we got to our new destination, called Kinveachey Lodge, I was saddened to learn that I was not allowed in and would have to sleep in the car. Still, I'm nothing if not adaptable and, perhaps, it was just as well. The main room was festooned with the heads of deer and other animals, some of them very harmless, and I might have been scared that mine would end up there in such a trigger-happy environment.

Being kept outside meant that I got more walks to relieve my boredom and there was a lot of bracken in which I could jump, following the scent of the deer which sometimes came on to the lawn. The bracken was full of black Argus butterflies and, as my instinct is to chase anything that flies, I had great fun with them. The Chap was always ribbing me because I never caught one but I would like to see him catch one with his mouth.

There were various lords in the fishing party but they were just like ordinary men. There was also the first real foreigner I had ever met – I don't count Americans – a jolly Austrian in leather breeches who used to romp round the lawn with me crying, '*Ja, ja* doggy, doggy! *Ja, ja,* doggy, doggy!'

My food was brought out to me by the Chap. One morning he brought me out some stuff called porridge. It was a bit salty but not bad. I understand that in Scotland there is a custom that you eat your porridge standing up. That posed no problem. I eat all my food standing up, though I enjoy sitting with a bone. Your food goes down under gravity but we have to do something about ours against gravity, at least for the first few inches. It is the same when we drink.

He also tried me with a haggis, which the Boss had bought in a shop in Grantown. That was much better. The shop had a haggis's nest in the window but that must have been a Scottish idea of a joke. An even bigger joke was the sight of the Boss emerging from the shop into the busy street in the big chest waders she could not be bothered to take off when we had left the river. All she needed was one of the big diver's helmets but nobody seemed to take any notice. When she had first emerged from the fishing hut wearing her huge waders and a floppy hat she suspected that I might not recognize her but I had no doubt, even for a second. Waders or not, the particular scent was still there.

Sadly, the Spey was so low that, during the whole week, hardly any of the fishers had any luck, even though some got up at five in the morning or fished in the gloaming until 9 p.m. Salmon fishing has been described as the art of casting a fly to a fish that isn't there and, that week, the anglers might as well have been fishing at home in the bath. The Chap says there is no worse news than the sad admission by a gillie – 'They're just nae there.' Even when they are there it is a mystery why they ever take a fly or bait, because they do not feed once they enter freshwater from the sea, being only interested in spawning. As the Chap says, it's like a man being offered a Mars Bar when he's closing in on some beautiful blonde. Still he goes on flogging away with his fly or bait when no dog or wolf would spend time trying to catch fish where there aren't any.

Happily for me, he does not believe in flogging away too long in the same place but likes to move about from one pool to another. Nobody can call him a man in the manger – the angler in a salmon pool who can't catch anything himself and is loath to move out to let anyone else try.

The only people who caught much on the Spey when we were there were the wretched pearl fishers who were able to reach water normally too deep for them to drag out the freshwater mussels. They knifed them all open, however small, in the hope that there might be a pearl inside for someone to wear. The banks were littered with their shells. Yet another example of the fearful combination of human vanity and greed.

The fishing was so bad that some of the party went to Loch Ness for the day in the hope of seeing the monster that is supposed to live in it. I wish we had gone because, if the monster comes ashore, it would leave a scent. They have failed to find it with ultrasonics, radar and other high-tech devices when a good tracker dog might have sniffed out its spoor.

Still, I had more good fun on the river bank because, apart from the water to paddle in, there were all sorts of birds. When the laird came I was kept in the car so that I could not put up the partridges in front of him, which, no doubt, I would have done and, in fact, did, after he had left. I did not, however, enjoy being dive-bombed by RAF fighter-bombers practising over the river.

At the end of the week, after all that travel, with all that tackle and the expenditure of all that effort and all that money by so many people only two little fish had been caught. I think I would have had more chance if I had been allowed to get in and grab one like the wolves and bears do in my ancestral Canada.

The only consolation was that the Boss won the sweep – £100 for guessing how many fish would be caught. She put the lowest number – seven – which could not have pleased the host very much and even that was five too many.

On our next Scottish trip we visited the Murthly and Glendelvine beat of the Tay to see the spot where Miss Ballantine, a gillie's daughter, achieved immortality by catching the record British salmon weighing 64 pounds, nearly seventy years ago. Her cottage is still there with the light on the chimney which she could put on if she was in trouble after she became badly arthritic. The Chap says that catching that fish was better than scoring 400 runs in a test match at Lords. She caught it on a bait and if only he could beat it with a salmon caught on a Dido – a fly made with hairs taken from my tail, with which he has caught some small ones – we would both then achieve immortality. It might also bring back some of those anglers who are going to Iceland, Russia and Alaska instead, with dire effects on the Scottish economy. Then some Scottish poet could celebrate my vital contribution in verse – 'Wee, modest chocolate-coated dog . . .'

The Chap had brought his rod and, with the gillie's assistance, he went through the motions of putting a Dido over the famous lie – by what is called the Bargie Stone – where the monster had been hooked nearly seventy years before. While he waded in waist deep I waited up to my hocks. I waited and watched in vain. There was no salmon of any size there or anywhere else on the beat so far as we could see. All have been killed off by the rapacious netsmen – at the mouth of the river as well as in the sea. So, next day, we went down to Perth to see them at their deadly slaughter. Using nylon nets which the salmon cannot see, and fishing day and night right across the river, the netsmen were raking in almost every fish that was trying to get up to spawn. The Chap was horrified and did his nut in the local paper where we were both pictured under the headline, 'A River in Ruins'. We were not popular with the netsmen!

Since then, and hopefully I had a paw in it, the worst nets have been removed and the Tay salmon should now have a better chance of survival, because the inroads made by anglers are relatively small. Sadly, though, resuscitation of the Scottish salmon stocks is likely to be so slow that neither the Chap nor I are likely to live to see it. Nevertheless, I still see him looking longingly at the huge fish in the glass cases in the billiards room at Kinnaird with thoughts, not entirely vain, I suppose, that he might one day fill the only space there with a 40-pounder. It would make my day and, I suspect, his life.

18 Bone-dreams

All dogs of action are dreamers

I have dwelt on our many canitarian and utilitarian contributions to human welfare in my first book and in this one, along with our beneficial impact on your culture, your literature, your sport and on your general well-being, both physical and mental. Many of you who are blind, deaf or otherwise disabled are dependent on us, as I have recounted. It is also self-evident that, by inducing their owners to take regular exercise, dogs reduce the risk of human heart ailments and improve fitness generally. Through companionship alone, they enhance the quality of life for millions, especially the lonely. Now, new research has shown that there is a further psychological 'spin-off' – in pet-owning families the relationship between children and their parents is better than in pet-less homes, leading to a happier family atmosphere.

As a result of my recent travels, with more evidence of such canine benefits and achievements coming my way, such feats make me wonder whether there is anything beyond our ambition, given the opportunity. What, then, should a progressive dog, like me, contemplate, constructively, in her bone-dreams? I do have my bone-dreams when I am gnawing gently away as a man would suck at a pipe. I might dream, for instance, that I have been named Dog of the Year, being honoured at the annual lunch at the Dogchester Hotel, with the guests enjoying bowls of wonderful food cooked by the master-chef, Mosidog. More excitingly I might dream of winning the Booker Prize with this book, being somewhat disappointed that I was not short-listed for the last one, considering the tawdry efforts of some who were. (Some female won it once with a book called *The Bone People* and I could certainly have made a better fist of that title!) Or I might dream of being in the Queen's Birthday Honours List as a DBE – Dog of the British Empire – though this no longer exists.

A personal letter which I received from Christina Foyle, who owns the famous London bookshop, congratulating me on my book, made me dream about being the guest of honour at one of her famous Literary Lunches to which she occasionally asks the Chap. Then there is my *Mastermind* dream. Once, when we came back from salmon fishing at Banchory, in Scotland, who should be in the hotel but the Chap's old friend, Magnus Magnusson. He made a fuss of me and this led to my bone-dreaming that I won the *Mastermind* trophy, sitting in that famous chair, with food as my specialized subject. There is one habit I share with Magnus – when I have started I always finish. Never once have I ever left anything in my bowl!

I might dream that I am a famous columnist in one of those papers owned by Rupert Murdog, *The Times*, for preference, or my photograph might appear in the *Sun*, for which I have more than the customary requirements. In fact, I am genuinely surprised that nobody has asked me to write a column because I overhear better political and social gossip than many journalists with famous names. People still tell the Chap all sorts of secrets and take no notice of me sitting there. While he may regard much of what we learn as too hot or too damaging to publish, I could take a different view – purely in the interest of press freedom and democracy, of course.

Recalling that an American dog, called Bosco, was recently elected Mayor of the Californian town of Sunol, I sometimes daydream of giving a similar service to human welfare. What occurred there was that, when two rather undistinguished men were thinking about putting up for Mayor, Bosco's owner claimed, 'My dog could beat the pair of you!' So, to settle the argument, there was an election and, indeed, the dog got the most votes, being eventually judged, when in office, 'a tough but fair politician'. This achievement inspired me to get the Chap to make enquiries about the possibility of standing for Mayor in this country but there were barriers which are insuperable, at least at the moment. As I have pointed out, dogs are classed as property in law and therefore cannot have citizenship which is necessary to stand for local or Parliamentary government.

I do not see why dogs should not have their own representatives in Parliament when we do so much for the community. It is surely wrong that only the human side of the argument should be heard when there is a canine crisis, like the awful business about 'killer dogs'. What a mess the politicians made of that! About 10,000 dogs were affected at the time, almost all Pit Bull Terriers. It became a criminal offence to keep a fighting dog in public without a muzzle and lead and no more may be imported. This was right and proper because Pit Bulls have been deliberately bred to be aggressive, fearless and so persistent in a fight that it is almost impossible to make them stop. However, following more harrowing incidents, some involving children, it became what the media called the 'Savage Dogs Crisis' and the Government's response was something of a panic measure amounting to canine murder – all fighting dogs would have to be destroyed. Why should dogs be subjected to automatic capital punishment for biting, when parents who kill their children after great brutality get no more than prison? And while media pictures of bitten children are terrible they are as nothing compared with the injuries inflicted on children by motor cars, which are ignored by the media photographers as being too horrific.

Under pressure from animal lovers the proposed law was modified so that from 1 December 1991 the dogs could be kept provided they were neutered. This was expected to reduce their aggressive instincts and also make it impossible for them to breed. I suspected that the Home Secretary made the destruction announcement first so that owners would be so relieved when he changed it to neutering that they would accept that without much fuss. However, the Chap says that politicians, whom he calls 'the dogs of jaw', are not that clever and do not think that far ahead.

Inevitably, the legislation against dangerous dogs backwashed on to other breeds. Strangers even looked scared of me if they encountered me on the tow-path. I suspect that, because of my colour, they thought that I couldn't be a Labrador and might be a Dobermann, especially if they spotted the 'Pincher' on my identity disc. The dogophobes seized on the opportunity. A little park near Newbury, where I was sometimes allowed a brief run, is now banned to dogs 'in the interest of the health of children', so the notice reads. Perhaps they will argue that the farmers should ban sheep and cattle from their fields because children, who might stray into them, might get sheep tick or mad cow disease. Nothing would surprise me with the anti-dog fanatics who are discriminating against a vulnerable minority – us.

There was a huge increase in the demand for muzzles for all manner of dogs. In fact, for a short time it became almost fashionable to be seen wearing a muzzle though I never spotted one on a Labrador. It was even said that Harrods were prepared to supply diamond-studded muzzles for very rich customers as they had provided diamond-studded collars in the past. Muzzling was, however, something of a nine-day wonder and it is a long time since I have seen a dog with any 'canine face furniture', as one newspaper called it.

I consider it every decent dog's duty to counter the evil reputation engendered by the canine crime wave by rebutting dogdom's bad publicity with constructive effort. Ask not, I declare, what dogdom can do for you: rather ask what you can do for dogdom. Where better could this voice be heard than in Parliament?

Actually, there is already a dog in the House of Commons, the cross-bred, Golden Retriever–Alsatian guide dog for the blind MP, David Blunkett, who sits with him there. I have a lot of sympathy with Offa, as he is called, for having to sit through all those speeches and all that raucous noise. Once, during the Chancellor's Budget Speech he was sick, and no wonder! Hopefully, he usually sleeps well there, as most dogs do when they are bored. He has nothing else to do because he cannot intervene even when canine interests are at stake.

Of course, one of the reasons why the quality of MPs is so poor is that brighter people will not put up with the long rigmarole of getting elected, sitting for years as lobby fodder on the back benches and then being chucked out in a general election. I would be prepared to make those sacrifices, provided I could continue writing, for I can see two tailor-made constituencies – Barking or the Isle of Dogs. To be the first dog to take my beanbag in the House of Commons would be a signal honour. I would take my constituency duties seriously, making a good paw of them by representing dogs as well as people and, unlike some human MPs, I would certainly not be there for pecuniary gain. I would be as honourable as the other members and more honourable than some. My private life would be above suspicion and my secretary would be in no danger. I would certainly enjoy the subsidized food. The only thing I would not like is the idea of the Whips.

The more I bone-dream about it the more I like the prospect of a political career. I would enjoy standing on my hind legs on the back benches, or even at the despatch-box, and any noise I voiced would be as constructive as that made by a lot of MPs, some of whom never speak at all. My maiden bark would certainly make the headlines. I would not just sit there growling 'hear hear' though I could enliven a good row, lending a different note to it. When it all became too boring I am sure that I could sleep there as soundly as the others do and I would look better if caught on television. I could certainly go through the voting lobby, when required, which is all that a lot of MPs do. I can see myself even casting the decisive vote – to the cry, 'The nose has it! The nose has it!'

I therefore induced the Chap to write to the Public Information Office in the Palace of Westminster to get an official ruling. After all, there is something of an historical precedent. The Roman Emperor, Caligula, sent his horse to the Upper Chamber by making him a senator. And the Chap assured me that I would certainly not be the first bitch in the House of Commons.

He wrote:

> A couple of years ago a dog was elected Mayor of a small American town and functioned to the satisfaction of the citizens, according to the *Daily Telegraph* which reported the matter, complete with a photograph of His Worship in his chains of office. In connection with a book I am researching I am making enquiries as to whether such an event would be possible here under the laws and customs of local government.
>
> As a corollary, could you please let me know whether there is anything in constitutional law to prevent a dog from standing for Parliament and, if so, what it is. Obviously, a dog could not take the oath if elected, but if one of the crackpot parties which now put up ridiculous candidates put up a dog, could anything be done to disqualify it in advance? Of one thing I am sure – a few hundred would vote for it!

As we expected, we received no reply probably because parliamentary officials, being so self-important, are also humourless. On the other hand, they may have discovered that dogs can stand for Parliament and wish to keep it secret, fearing a flood of candidates.

While a canine MP may not be possible now, one never knows what the future may hold if I persist. If people can stand for organizations like the Monster Raving Loonies and other crackpot parties, why shouldn't I found one and stand as a candidate? I can put up the deposit from my bank account and could lose it with equanimity, having dispensed with so many deposits in the past. In accordance with the election rules, the TV newsreaders would have to mention my party and, while dogs can't vote at the moment, dog lovers can and a lot might vote for me.

Meanwhile, the only thing for me to do is to press for parliamentary reform as the suffragettes did. Perhaps I could get the Chap to chain me to a lamppost. When David Blunkett first tried to enter the Palace of Westminster with a guide dog, before he became an MP, he was told that dogs were barred. But after a campaign this ruling was reversed. So I will persist with mine. Meanwhile, it will remain a bone-dream like my eventual elevation to the House of Lords. That monster beanbag called the Woolsack looks very comfortable.

I must say that I would enjoy being addressed as Lady Dido and Your Dogship, as many bitches would. Then I might be granted a coat of arms which, perhaps, in my case, should be a coat of legs. Instead of dog 'supporters', which are commonly shown holding up the heraldic shield, I could have the Chap and the Boss. No doubt, like any dog's, my lineage would have the odd bar sinister, way back, with a few Fitzdidos as a result. As for my motto, with my enthusiasm and zest for life, I would settle for 'What's next?' – in dog latin, of course – 'Quid proximus?'

Again, to indulge me, the Chap wrote to the College of Arms on this controversial matter:

> Last year I ghosted a book for my chocolate Labrador, Dido, called *One Dog and Her Man*. We are now busy with Dido's next book and in it she deals with the effects of the fame which authorship and publicity has brought her. Musing on the future, she expresses the

wish to have her own coat of arms if this were possible, in a man-dominated world.

There seems to be only one way to settle her doubts – to ask the College whether there is anything in its constitution to prevent a dog from having armorial bearings and, if so, what is it? If no such bar exists perhaps we could pursue the matter further.

In due course we received a charming letter from the Chester Herald, Hubert Chesshyre, who happened to be the Officer in Waiting during the week when our letter arrived. He explained that, since the Middle Ages, arms are granted by more senior heralds who are known as Kings of Arms. They are empowered to grant arms to 'eminent men' but this also includes women and corporate bodies. So I am not excluded by sex. However, Mr Chesshyre does not think that 'men' could be stretched to include dogs (even the royal Corgis) however eminent they or their owners might be. He added, 'I will gladly approach the Kings of Arms on Dido's behalf but if, as I suspect, they consider that she lacks the necessary qualifications for an official grant I may be able to provide something for her under the counter, though this would involve her in a little expense.'

So, with money being so tight these days, it would seem that the only coat of arms I shall ever get is the one also covering my legs. But the idea of the Chap and the Boss as my supporters remains a perennially delightful dream.

I am more than pleased with my real-life lot for I have realized the most important dreams a dog can have. Every time that we pass the kennels of the Canine Defence League in the next village, Hamstead Marshall, where there are scores of stray or abandoned dogs waiting for homes, I appreciate how fortunate I am with a caring pack and buoyant health. Nevertheless, dreams cost nothing and dogs and humans alike must have them. So I shall bone-dream on.

19 A Thinking Dog's Creed

Go, like the Indian, in another life,
Expect thy dog, thy bottle and thy wife

In my previous book, in a chapter entitled 'Can Eternity Belong to Me?', I spoke out for all non-human creatures who are denied entry to Paradise. The theological wisdom which the Chap and I received at that time, from various sources, indicated that neither dogs nor any other animals could enter Paradise because we do not possess souls and without a soul there is nothing to 'pass over'. So all those other animals associated so strongly with the Christian faith – the lamb, the donkey, St Jerome's lion and the doves of peace – are barred. Even the birds of Paradise are denied entry along with my poor old friend George, the canary, who looked in fine nick and in full song one day, then off colour the next and dead in three days, showing how tenuous life is in spite of all the efforts by the Boss and the Chap to save him.

What was the good of St Francis preaching to the birds if they had no immortal souls? With no songbirds in Heaven no wonder those angels are always sounding off on their trumpets and their harps. And what about all those cases of dog apparitions being seen by humans? If there is any truth in those it must be support for an after-life and therefore for a soul. It also seems to me monstrously unjust that there is to be no compensation for the sufferings which so many animals, including some dogs, endure in this world while humans, who feel they have had a raw deal here, can look forward to eternal bliss.

However, just as my first book was going to press the present Pope, John Paul II, made a statement which some Catholic animal lovers had interpreted as suggesting that the old teaching might have been wrong and that we might have souls after all. The Chap determined to follow this up, not only in my interests and that of my fellow dogs, but in his own because if there are no dogs in Heaven he doesn't want to go there, even if it were remotely possible that he might be invited. He had a nodding acquaintance with the Catholic Church's chief representative in Britain, the Archbishop of Westminster, Cardinal Basil Hume (whose real name is George), because they once received honorary degrees together. I see the Cardinal's picture every day because there is a colour photograph of the two of them in their gaudy glad rags in one of the loos. So he decided to seek guidance and an opinion there.

Being a stickler for 'doing his homework' the Chap looked the Cardinal up in *Who's Who* and cried, 'This looks promising, Dido! Before he became Archbishop he was Professor of Dogmatic Theology!' In spite of that specific expertise, he did not get much of a response. The Cardinal was not to be drawn on such a controversial issue – at least in print. A few days later we found out why. A body called the Catholic Study Circle for Animal Welfare had clashed with him because he had categorically stated that, in his view, dogs and other animals did not have souls, which means that if he becomes the next Pope, as has been mooted as possible, there will be no change in the dog dogma. I gather that he has since had a few nasty letters from dog and cat lovers because an essential ingredient of belief in the next world for many people is the confidence in being reunited with those they love which, surely, includes their dogs and cats.

The Study Circle, which cannot bring itself to believe that loving and lovable creatures like dogs are soulless, had latched on to the Pope's statement which indicated to them that animals might share eternity. One spokesperson thought it was appalling that, in the last century, some Italian archbishop had ruled that because a dog does not have a soul it is not sinful to beat it or do anything else with it. The same reasoning explained why it was not sinful for humans to slaughter animals for food or even for sport. According to some theologians the 'brutes', as they call all us animals, were specially created for humans – for their use, service and pleasure and to do whatever they like with them. In fact, some humans should be given the dog-o'-nine-tails for offences they have committed against 'God's creatures'.

Earlier civilizations, like Red Indians, had been more enlightened, treating animals as fellow creatures in the tapestry of nature, entitled to respect and conservation to such a degree that they were almost apologetic when killing them for food or clothing. In ancient Egypt, the dog was sacred and to kill one was a capital offence. In Persia, the dog was held in special honour and to deprive one of food was a serious crime. Very sensible! Unfortunately the prophet Mahomet ruined things for us in those parts by saying, 'Angels will not enter a house containing a dog.' He added 'or pictures', thereby depriving the Muslim world of much of the art which

Muslim painters might have contributed as well as the companionship of dogs. I suppose I had better be careful what I say or I might get a 'fatwa' condemning me to death and would have to have a bodyguard at the public expense. Fortunately, I know a very nice Arab who is descended from the prophet and has bought several copies of my first book so, perhaps, he would intercede.

Though all our sympathies were with the Study Circle it clearly did not carry much theological clout so the Chap decided to follow the principle he had always applied in such circumstances – to go right to the top. He wrote to the Vatican, in Rome, a move which had my immediate support. It seemed only fitting that such a challenging problem should be considered by the highest conclave of the oldest Church.

Eventually we received a reply from the Secretariat of State signed by Monsignor Sepe, the 'Assessor', on beautiful paper watermarked with the Pope's insignia, the triple tiara and the crossed keys of St Peter. He said that, during a public audience, the present Pope had affirmed that animals, like people, were given 'the breath of life' by God. He had then added, 'also the animals possess a soul and that men (and presumably women) must love and feel solidarity with our smaller brethren.' He then said that animals 'are as near to God as men are.' All that sounded most promising for dogs, though perhaps not for elephants or giraffes which can hardly count as 'smaller brethren', but then came the crunch. Monsignor Sepe said that he had consulted further and had found that while the Catholic Church taught that animals do have souls they do not have *immortal* souls!

This, the Monsignor insisted, was all that the Pope had meant and he dismissed the views of Catholic theologians 'in certain circles' who interpreted the Pope's words in other ways as being 'wishful thinking'.

This seems to be a fudge and a fiddle to me. Two kinds of souls? First-class and second-class souls? Any self-respecting dog would dismiss it as gobbledepooch. Is there any limit to human ingenuity to keep us out of Paradise? What is the good of a soul if it is not immortal? And if the soul of a dog is not 'immortal', what happens to it? Does it die like the body? I always thought that the whole point about a soul was that it was not destroyed at death. Clearly, the whole thing is splitting whiskers and I think that the Vatican has got itself into a philosophical mess. No statement is too absurd for some philosopher to make.

At a big country dinner in a marquee, at which I was allowed to be present, the Chap raised the issue with an elderly vicar of the Church of England who was seated next to him. At first the vicar said that he believed that animals did have immortal souls but when he heard what the Vatican had said he sided with the Catholics. Obviously he had never given it much thought. Very disappointing! As the argument developed the vicar insisted that, according to the Bible, all other living things, including me, had been put on earth solely for man's use and that animals, being only 'things' with no reason and no free will, cannot have any rights. As they have no rights, people have no duties towards them, he argued. The Chap made it clear that he had never heard such junk. He assured that vicar that I had plenty of free will which I frequently expressed by making choices. Further, I was as much entitled to the Rights of Dog as he was to the Rights of Man. And if there was no after-life for me then I, and other animals, should be treated with special consideration in our short lives here rather than exploited. As to every living thing being on earth solely for man's use, how did he account for the

AIDs virus, the plague, sharks, tigers and other living things which kill him? And how did he explain the undeniable fact that thousands of species of animals, like the dinosaurs, had lived on earth for millions of years and had become extinct long before man appeared on the scene to 'make use' of them? The vicar had no sensible answers and in his confusion knocked over his glass of red wine creating an awful mess, which I thought might have been deliberate to cause a change of subject. Anyway, it did me a bit of good because a plate of ham was ruined by the wine and the Chap saw that I got it. Fortunately, the vicar did not know that the Chap was a keen game-shot and a fisherman or he might have been able to riddle his virtuous stance.

More seriously though, this belief, stated in Genesis, that man is set apart from all other forms of life and that the whole of nature has been created for his use is having catastrophic effects. It has sanctioned man's aggressive instinct to exploit everything, living and inanimate, without thought for the future, with science and technology being the tools for the onslaught. It underlies the menacing effects of pollution, the over-exploitation of the forests, agricultural land and the rivers and seas. For this to cease, or at least be reduced to more sensible proportions, there must be a return to the older and more humble belief that man is just part of nature with all the creatures in it being intricately related and mutually dependent. While man has the power to exploit the rest he will continue to do so at his peril.

Obviously, I have entered a theological minefield but, Pope or no Pope, Cardinal or no Cardinal, the Catholic Study Circle for Animal Welfare continues to be sure that animals do have proper, full-blown souls and that, being incapable of sin because they do not understand what it is, dogs and other animals must be very pleasing to their Creator and, so, may well be let into Paradise, which is encouraging. They even accuse the Vatican of 'species-ism' a form of discrimination like racism and sexism.

I find it hard to believe that there is a separate Paradise for animals but if there is and there are no humans there I, for one, do not want to go, though I can see that the millions of animals which have been persecuted by man would be delighted at the prospect. Further, it has occurred to me that there could be no real bones in any Paradise because something would have to die there to provide them and that, surely, could never happen.

Meanwhile I can see why the Vatican is loath to admit that we might have immortal souls. One of the objections to murder is sending a soul into the next world before its time, a human life being sacred until the Almighty decides that it should end. So would we begin to hear about the sanctity of canine life if we had immortal souls? And how would this affect the human practice of putting down unwanted dogs – 1,000 a day in Britain alone, I am told? I should like to hear more of the sanctity of dog.

A ruling that animals have immortal souls would not be popular with the customers of butchers and might increase the number of vegetarians. I have been told about an old lady, with not long to live, who was pleading with her vicar to assure her that her cat would be in Heaven with her. Finally he said, 'Well, what you have to realize is that if your cat is there so will be the turkey you ate for Christmas.' The cat might welcome her but the turkey . . .

It also follows that if dogs have souls, then so have foxes. So where does this leave fox-hunting and how are the hounds placed, helping to send their cousins to wherever it is that foxes go, if they go anywhere? If creatures were deemed to have souls the impact of such a pronouncement on all blood sports could be disastrous. Imagine the reaction of the bull-fighting fraternity in Catholic Spain or that of the bird-shooters in Italy! Even fish would have to be included because there is no cut-off point on the evolutionary ladder where anyone can say, 'This is where souls begin.' The soul of a sole would be an intriguing topic for the rarer altitudes of philosophy and theology.

Then there would be the question of Judgement Day. All those canine resurrections! Would dogs that died as pups remain as pups for eternity? Would dogs that died when old and decrepit remain that way for ever? In the paintings showing saints in Heaven they are mostly bearded, bald and wrinkled old men, way past their prime. A lot of people get fed up with life when they reach that stage. Why punish saints – or dogs – by keeping them in that condition for ever? As there seems to be a penalty to pay for every advantage, perhaps the one for having a long life in this world is remaining decrepit in the next.

As I pointed out in my first book, it would not just be a question of dogs and humans on Judgement Day. All the other animals would be there – all those that have ever existed, including the dinosaurs. If this earth is overpopulated, what would Heaven be like? According to common human belief, a lot of humans will not qualify for Paradise because of their sinful behaviour on earth, but as animals do not know what sin is we would all qualify, while those of your lot who failed would descend to the eternal flames.

Of course, if you accept that man is just an animal at the top of the evolutionary ladder, you may not believe in the existence of souls at all. If, instead, you believe in Adam and Eve, you can assume, as the Bible suggests, that they were the first creatures to have immortal souls. But if you are convinced, as the Chap is, that *Homo sapiens* descended from less advanced, more ape-like creatures then you are stuck with deciding at what point in time man's ancestors acquired a soul. I have to say that nobody has been able to tell either me or the Chap what a soul really is. All they say is that it is something invisible and intangible which survives the body and lives on after death. I am not even sure that it is invisible because I sometimes hear the Chap say to the Boss, when we have been alone on the river, 'I didn't see a soul.'

The Chap can see no evidence for the soul's existence and, without souls there can be no after-life. As he puts it, this life is all there is and it is not a dress rehearsal. I suspect that this is one of the reasons why the Chap will never waste a minute and tries to get as much enjoyment out of life as possible, as, of course, I do anyway. It is certainly better than the attitude of some humans who regard life as just a pointless and rather wearisome march to the knackeryard. So, should I just trust in dog and do the right? I think, perhaps, that it is wiser, safer and more reassuring to back it both ways and assume that Paradise might exist.

Meanwhile, on that, perhaps depressing, subject I heard about a lord who has recently erected a gravestone in his stately home's dog cemetery featuring crossed bones and a tin of pet food and the deeply carved name Old Smelly, which I feel sure was not the deceased's real name. If only His Lordship knew how he reeked to his dog, with its highly refined sense of smell, he might not have been so unkind. Any of us would be justified in memorializing a master as Old Stinker but we could not be so heartless.

I have given some thought to what I would like in the shape of a memorial. I think I'd like one of those medieval-style tombs where there would be a sculpted figure of me lying on my back staring into space and with my rear paws resting on a miniature figure of the Chap, crouching. Yes, the more I think about it the more appealing the idea becomes.

Meanwhile, I have been giving thought to a way of life for dogs rather than a way of death – a thinking dog's creed, a sensible code of behaviour for dealing with our predicament in this world. Perhaps other dogs, and their owners, might care to profit from a few principles which life has taught me, though, as with the Chap and his principles, I am not always able to follow them. So, if I may appoint myself as a spokesbitch I would suggest the following canine commandments:

Be faithful to the pack. Reliability is a prime virtue for dogs as well as humans.

Be around. Make the rest of the pack feel deprived and worried where you might be if you are not in view. Few men would relish a wife who would prefer that her husband was never out of her sight but with a dog it is a compliment.

Be useful and pull your weight. Actions speak louder than growls. For my part, I am more than a companion. I'm a guard dog, a fishing dog and a literary dog.

Never withhold your affection, even if you are poorly treated. Always lick the hand that feeds you but, in general, try to be even-pawed with your affections, which will then be reciprocated. In the dog world it pays to be loved by several people rather than by only one, though, in the human world that can cause problems.

As regards other people – and other dogs – bark as you find. Be honest, but foster the illusions of the other members of the pack, especially the human ones.

Do not necessarily expect fairness and justice, but be strong on forgiveness, of which there is more in our nature than in man's. Forgive the most those whom you love the most.

Never forget that we live in a dangerous world which contains many dog haters and that the politicians may align themselves with them rather than with us because they have votes and we don't. When the Dangerous Dogs Act came in on 12 August 1991 (with the grouse) some of these dogophobes immediately tried to get it extended to cover more than the four breeds it stipulated.

Give and take in both mutual fellowship and dogship. Like a man's life, a dog's is about compromise. Try to create options, either of which will give you pleasure.

Always be enthusiastic. To some dogs, as with some people, life is just one big yawn. But be your age. When I was a pup I barked as a pup, I understood as a pup, I thought as a pup: but when I became a bitch I put away puppish things. Some dogs don't.

Don't overdo one-updogship. Gloat in private when you have been proved right, for instance, when you have been accused of barking at nothing and they finally realize that there really is someone at the door. Some dogs make the mistake of treating their owners like animals when, at all times, we must remember that they are only human.

Try not to be too demanding though I appreciate that this is sometimes difficult. Take joy in simplicity for which there is much to be said. Don't be misled by trappings.

Some dogs, like some people, complicate their lives unnecessarily. Give the impression that you are happy in the smallness of your needs. Once I have been fed and walked all I ask is somewhere quiet and warm to lie. (As all dogs know, there are some days when the most sensible thing to do is to stay in bed. We can often do that when humans can't.)

Don't push your luck. Stand on your own four paws but don't overdo it. Who dares does not necessarily win in the dog world but who cares usually does. Some dogs have a self-destructive streak which ruins their lives.

Never begrudge another dog its luck. You never know what the paw of fate has in store, even for those it appears to favour. (I've noticed that you often get your bad luck when you are doing a good turn for somebody else.)

Never fight below your weight – one of the Chap's guiding principles – meaning do not bother yourself with any kind of conflict with individuals, dogs or humans, who are beneath your dignity.

Try to avoid social gaffes, though I sometimes fail on that score when, for instance, my affectionate temperament overcomes my natural reserve and I jump up. Or, at night, I might lick one the Chap's caps to shabbiness – out of sheer love for him when he is out of my sight, though it does give them character. Still, the dog–man relationship has taught me that it is pointless to expect anything like perfection – the state of being without defect or fault – from dog or man.

Finally, don't tell the humans all our canine secrets. Bark it not in Bath nor murmur it in the streets of Ashby-de-la-Zouch. Retain some degree of mystery but learn all you can about their secret lives.

Thus barked Didothustra!

Epilogue

Escape me? Never!

The Boss promised me that on publication day of *A Box of Chocolates* she would invite some of our mutual friends and open a double bottle of champagne to make it into a *magnum opus*. I suspect that as the abstemious Chap sips his orange juice he will also be quietly drinking to the cessation of our literary partnership to enable him to return to writing about purely human issues. I fear that he has another think coming. The particular pleasure of dog authorship has penetrated to my bones. I feel sure that I have still more documentary books in me and there are my memoirs which could be far more revealing about the Chap than his own. I could many a tale unfold and probably will. Further, at the age of five and with my pups behind me, my career as a canine journalist and newshound has barely begun. I might even try fiction – like *Dog on a Hot Tin Roof* or *Dog and Superdog*.

As the Chap has had so many near brushes with death in his charmed life I sense that he has long suspected that he was being preserved for some special purpose. I must convince him that my books are it and get my publisher to put pressure on him. He has not been reduced to writing about dogs, in my opinion, but substantially elevated, especially now that spies are a busted flush.

Queen Victoria's last word as she expired, wondering what her wayward son might do to the Realm, was, 'Bertie!' Citizen Kane's was, 'Rosebud!' I have a feeling that the Chap's will be, 'Dido!'

THE END

ONE DOG AND HER MAN

by Dido, assisted by Chapman Pincher

Chapman Pincher, distinguished writer on spies and the world's intelligence services, is also the owner of a rather special chocolate Labrador bitch called Dido. Or is it Dido who owns 'her Chap', as she refers to her human companion?

Here in Dido's autobiography, ghosted by Chapman Pincher, we are given an insight into an intimate and loving relationship. Trained as a zoologist, Chapman Pincher is in an ideal position to interpret Dido's view of the world and share her wisdom with other dogs and dog owners. Dido has much to say about herself, as one would expect in an autobiography, but reveals almost as much about 'her chap' in this touching and eloquent tribute to canine culture.

'Fascinating and hilarious' *Daily Mail*

A Bantam Paperback

0 553 40439 3

A DOG'S LIFE IN THE DALES

by Katy Cropper

Wensleydale, Swaledale, Hardraw, Great Shunner, Dodd Fell – these evocative Yorkshire names are the hills, valleys and villages where Katy Cropper lives, walks and works with her dogs and sheep. And there in the Dales, this young shepherdess might have stayed undiscovered by the public at large, had she not become the popular 1990 winner of the prestigious *One Man and His Dog* competition in front of seven million TV viewers – the first and only time it has been won by a woman.

In this frank, funny and often moving self-portrait, Katy cheerfully admits that while she is sometimes too frisky for humans to handle, she has always been happy with animals. She candidly describes her first disastrous attempts at sheepdog trialling in North Wales, when she would vainly shout with increasing desperation at her dog, Sykes, as he headed off into the distance, without the least interest in finding some sheep. She then formed a much more successful trainer-dog relationship with her Border Collie, Lad, despite his apparent handicap of having lost one leg in an accident.

Sykes, Lad and Trim, who helped Katy win the *One Man and His Dog* trophy, her other dogs, the sheep, her ducks and all her other animals – they are the real stars of her book. But coming a close second are the human characters that inhabit Katy's world in the Dales. They are all part of the day-to-day and seasonal living, which she has caught perfectly, both in words and in the appealing pencil drawings, with which she illustrates her book.

A Bantam Paperback

0 553 40638 8

A SELECTION OF NON-FICTION TITLES
PUBLISHED BY BANTAM AND CORGI BOOKS

THE PRICES SHOWN BELOW WERE CORRECT AT THE TIME OF GOING TO PRESS. HOWEVER TRANSWORLD PUBLISHERS RESERVE THE RIGHT TO SHOW NEW RETAIL PRICES ON COVERS WHICH MAY DIFFER FROM THOSE PREVIOUSLY ADVERTISED IN THE TEXT OR ELSEWHERE.

All Corgi/Bantam Books are available at your bookshop or newsagent, or can be ordered from the following address:
Corgi/Bantam Books,
Cash Sales Department,
P.O. Box 11, Falmouth, Cornwall TR10 9EN

UK and B.F.P.O. customers please send a cheque or postal order (no currency) and allow £1.00 for postage and packing for the first book plus 50p for the second book and 30p for each additional book to a maximum charge of £3.00 (7 books plus).

Overseas customers, including Eire, please allow £2.00 for postage and packing for the first book plus £1.00 for the second book and 50p for each subsequent title ordered.

NAME (Block Letters) ....

ADDRESS ....

....